THE
GLOUCESTER
RUGBY
MISCELLANY

ROBERT HARRIS

The History Press

In memory of Cath, still my inspiration.

First published 2012, this edition 2014

The History Press
The Mill, Brimscombe Port
Stroud, Gloucestershire, GL5 2QG
www.thehistorypress.co.uk

© Robert Harris, 2012, 2014

The right of Robert Harris to be identified as the Author
of this work has been asserted in accordance with the
Copyrights, Designs and Patents Act 1988.

British Library Cataloguing in Publication Data.
A catalogue record for this book is available from the British Library.

ISBN 978 0 7509 5468 6

Typesetting and origination by The History Press
Printed in Great Britain

ACKNOWLEDGEMENTS

My sincere thanks are due to the many Gloucester Rugby greats who helped make this book possible. Without exception, their class on the field was matched by their class off it.

FOREWORD

by Mike Teague

There were family connections with Gloucester through my uncle Colin, and I used to go to games with my dad. I suppose my earliest recollection of Kingsholm is of my uncle Colin running out in front of me for a midweek game in miserable weather and slapping this bloke on the back. It wasn't a thump, it was a proper rugby slap and it made a distinctive noise. It seems like one minute I was playing locally and the next I was running out for the United.

Those who watch Gloucester understand rugby. Honesty on the field is applauded but they can spot someone who shirks or who is not so honest. That's when you hear the rhetoric of the Shed. Personally, I was always grateful for the support I received.

I think I was lucky to be involved with the club at a wonderful time when there was a wonderful group of players. There is no better club in the world to play for than Gloucester on a good day because rugby is the biggest thing in the city.

FIRST EVER GAME

Gloucester Rugby Club was formed in 1873 following a meeting in the city at the Spread Eagle Hotel. Francis Hartley, who previously played for the London-based club Flamingoes, helped assemble a team to take on the college school who, coincidentally, played on the Kingsholm field that Gloucester now call home.

PHIL BLAKEWAY'S FOUR RETIREMENTS

Front-row forward Phil Blakeway broke his neck playing for Gloucester in a midweek game against South Wales Police at Kingsholm in 1977, but his injury was not fully diagnosed until the following weekend – after he had played for Gloucestershire against Cornwall in Camborne.

The greengrocer from Tewkesbury went on to become a key figure in England's 1980 Grand Slam-winning team.

Blakeway actually retired four times in his career. He initially retired in 1977 following that broken neck, then in 1981 because of a back problem. Retirement number three came in 1982, but he quit for real in 1985 because of further neck and back problems.

As a youngster he wanted to be a modern pentathlete rather than a rugby player. He was named as a reserve for the World Junior Championships in 1968 and trained with Robbie Phelps, who was established in the British modern pentathlon team. He began taking rugby seriously when he joined Cheltenham as a speedy young full-back.

TWO LAPS AROUND THE PITCH
AND A BATH

Now 86, Ken Daniell is one of Gloucester's oldest surviving players. Ken scored more than 50 tries in a relatively short career which was cut short by a serious knee injury at the age of 24.

Also a talented sprinter, he made his Gloucester debut in 1945 as the club struggled to rebuild after the Second World War.

'It was tough getting going,' he recalled. 'Harold Boughton ran the side when I first went down to Kingsholm, but we were a social side. We met twice a week for training, which was generally two laps of the pitch, then a bath. We were a tight group. The game was so different; the forwards would put the ball on the floor and dribble it down the field while we stood and watched.'

Ken's father played for Gloucester in the 1920s. Daniell Junior took up rugby playing for his works team, Atlas, but quickly made an impression at Gloucester, serving as vice-captain in 1949/50 to Gordon Hudson.

He said: 'The best I played with were half-backs Danny Evans and Willie Jones. Willie was marvellous, very clever and a superb kicker. My most memorable game was against Cardiff. It was absolutely packed out and there were people sat inside the railings on the side of the pitch. Going to Cardiff was lethal because we'd get terrible stick off their supporters. Some players would back out but one who never did was Digger Morris. He got more stick than anyone but he seemed to love it and I don't think he ever missed a game in Cardiff.'

CAN WE HAVE OUR BALLS BACK?

In 1954 Garth and Godfrey Cromwell became the club's first ball boys. They got 2s per game, providing they retrieved all of the balls. That meant knocking on plenty of doors in the streets surrounding Kingsholm. Garth went on to become a top referee and even took charge of matches at Gloucester.

BIZARRE TWIST OF FATE

Gordon Sargent's decision not to go on tour with Lydney resulted in him becoming captain of Gloucester. Sarge played more than 200 games for Gloucester in his career but in 1982, at the age of 32, he opted to return to his hometown club Lydney. At the end of that 1982 season, Lydney went on tour to America but Sarge didn't want to go. Peter Jones, the young Gloucester prop, went instead of him, with Sarge agreeing to provide front-row cover for Gloucester in their final 2 games of the season. He ended up playing in both matches and the players lobbied him to captain them the following season.

He stayed with Gloucester until his retirement at the age of 38. Sargent made his only appearance for England as a replacement in a rare win in Ireland. Ironically, the man he came on for that day was his Gloucester team-mate Phil Blakeway. As well as all those appearances for Gloucester, Sargent also played 358 times for Lydney.

THE HARD MAN'S HARD MAN

Many who played alongside him rate Jack Fowke as one of the hardest men ever to pull on a cherry and white shirt. But who does Jack rate as the toughest opponent he ever faced?

'That would be John O'Shea, the former Cardiff and Newbridge prop,' said Jack.

Jack started life as a hooker with Stroud but played primarily at loosehead prop for Gloucester from 1959 to 1970. His brother Roy (whose son Bobby also represented Gloucester) and brother-in-law Ron Pitt played for Gloucester during the same era.

Though rock-hard on the pitch, Jack showed his soft side by giving plenty of encouragement to young up-and-coming props such as Mike Burton, Keith Richardson and Robin Cowling. Jack said: 'Keith was a back-row when he joined us but he was keen to learn. I remember Mickey Burton when he started out at about 18. He was a very good scrummager and had a bit of flair. I was happy to help anyone who wanted to learn with a few tips.'

Incredibly, Jack says he never received any formal coaching. 'I just learnt as I went on; I soon worked out where to put my arms and what to do. Don Rutherford made you think about the game but I'm not sure he understood much about scrummaging. Scrummaging used to be a bigger part of the game. Personally, I think the old game was better, to me the modern game is more like rugby league. Some of the arts of forward play have died out. I enjoyed my time at Gloucester. When I first went down there we got a bottle of beer and two beer vouchers for the White Hart – three if you were lucky. Our kit was supplied but we had to pay for our own boots.'

PAUL WEBB ON THE PERKS OF
BEING AN AMATEUR

'The difference between playing for the firsts and seconds in my day was that in the firsts you got a 22-gallon barrel of beer after the match and chicken and chips. In the seconds it was an 11-gallon barrel of beer with sausage and chips.'

Paul Webb played for Gloucester from 1982 to 1985 and also represented England Colts. He says his most memorable game was versus Auckland at Kingsholm.

'It was so foggy we should never have played,' he said. 'We ran out to applause then there was silence because no one could see us. During the game we got a cheer on the stand side and another on the Shed side. Otherwise, the whole match was played in virtual silence.'

UNITED GO ON STRIKE
FOR A FULL TEAM

Harold Symonds joined Gloucester from All Blues in 1959 and played for the club until 1972. He captained the United team in 1972, a successful season in which many emerging stars were blooded. One of the young men Harold remembers most fondly from that era is Phil Blakeway, who he rates as the toughest man he saw on a rugby field.

He said: 'Off the pitch Phil was, and still is, an absolute gent, one of the nicest men you will ever meet. But on a rugby pitch he was different. I can't remember how many times I was pulled aside as captain by the referee and told "please control Blakeway".'

Harold joined Gloucester as a tall 6ft 2in centre – a rarity in the 1950s. Within a few weeks he realised he wasn't going to make it as a centre and was all set to return to All Blues, until Roy Sutton encouraged him to stay as a wing forward.

Harold said: 'The club was very different in the 1950s and '60s. The committee was friendly and very hands-on. I wouldn't say training was ad hoc but it was not structured or disciplined. Dare I say it, players in the 1950s played mainly to keep fit. Don Rutherford helped to change things and got us playing seriously. We were often accused of playing 10-man rugby – people said our three-quarters only went along for the ride. Obviously you play to your strengths, but we had some quick guys too. Terry Hopson could slice through any gap when he was on his mettle, but he could be a moody player. Mickey Booth and Terry were outstanding half-backs. We could be on our 25 and Terry would send a superb kick down the field, which would drop just short of their line. I'd run down the pitch past the opposition's forwards and hear them cursing "Flaming Hopson's done it again!"'

Harold is often accused of being the man who took Gloucester out on strike in the early 1960s. He explained: 'The United side back then often found themselves going away – especially over the Severn Bridge into Wales – with 13 or 14 players and it was embarrassing to be getting off the coach at places like Cardiff and Newport and having to ask the locals if they fancied a game. One day we were going into Wales and we had 13 men. I thought this is stupid so I said "I'm going over to the White Hart, if you get 15 come and get me." However, all of the players treated me like a trade union leader and followed me. It hit the press that Gloucester had gone on strike and I got a severe reprimand from the committee, although I think one or two like Digger Morris were secretly behind me. It had a positive effect in that a secretary was appointed to the United team and we didn't go short after that.'

SMALLPOX STOPS PLAY

In 1895/96 several matches were cancelled due to a smallpox epidemic in the city.

MOGGY IDOLISED GORDON BANKS

It's hard to believe but Richard Mogg, one of Gloucester's all-time best backs, didn't take up rugby at any level until he was 16. Within two years he was playing for Gloucester's firsts. He explained: 'I played football at school and for Parry Hall. I supported Stoke City, still do, and although I wasn't a goalkeeper, Gordon Banks was my hero. I didn't like rugby at school. I was too small. I didn't even play for the school team.'

Mogg drifted into rugby when a few of the lads he hung around with started playing for Tredworth. The club launched a colts team just for them, but they hardly won a game and most of the players packed up within a year or two as the team folded. Mogg stood out, however, and began playing for Tredworth's senior team. By 1974 he was playing for Gloucester. He recalled those early days at Kingsholm, saying: 'I made my debut versus Cheltenham and remember looking around the changing room at all these great internationals like Peter Butler and John Watkins. The week before, I had been playing on the Lannet [Tredworth's ground]. Peter Butler was very good to me, he looked after me, but everyone seemed a lot older than I was. I pulled on my cherry and white shirt, this long-haired kid, and it was way too big for me. I don't know what I weighed then, but I was never more than 13½ stones at any time in my career. Playing for Gloucester was a dream come true but I never ever thought I'd play 510 times.'

Mogg soon realised he had to toughen up to survive at Kingsholm. That applied to everyone. He said: 'When Richard Pascall first joined us we called him a few names. Someone would be lying offside and he'd be shouting "ref, he's offside!" Everyone else knew that if you were on the floor on the wrong side you'd get some aluminium.'

Mogg started out on the wing, but played primarily in the centre. He scored the winning try in the 1978 John Player Cup final, but says beating Gosforth that year in the same competition was an even better result.

'The crowd for that game was enormous. We were trying to shout moves and couldn't hear ourselves. There's a lot of pressure playing in front of a big Kingsholm crowd like that.'

Mogg once scored six tries in a match versus Guy's Hospital, but it doesn't rate highly among his personal list of achievements. He said: 'To be honest, they were that poor I think a local side would have beaten them. Sometimes we used to play against sides knowing beforehand we would win. Some of our opponents just liked the prestige of playing Gloucester. Derbies against local sides were often tougher. We lost to Stroud and had some tough Thursday nights down at Lydney. They were lovely people down there but they did like to get stuck in.'

Mogg believes there were more flair players about in his era than today. He added: 'I admired people like Gerald Davies and David Duckham; it would be interesting to see how they'd cope today. I rated Bob Clewes, too. He wasn't known for his pace but he scored a lot of tries because he was so good at reading the game.

'I think there are flair players still about, just not so many. It's more about size and power today because there's less space. I rate Charlie Sharples though.'

When his Gloucester career was over, Mogg played a season for Cheltenham before returning to the place where it all started, Tredworth. He said: 'Tredworth were always good to me, I wanted to give something back. I played socially. I still enjoyed my rugby but the pace and strength was going. In Gloucester everybody knows everybody and Tredworth RFC has been a big part of my life. I lived just over the road.

'I'm happy with what I achieved in the game and the honours I got. I had a final trial for England but never got a cap. I probably wasn't quite good enough.'

DID YOU KNOW?

The Revd Bill Phillips, one of three clergymen to play for Gloucester in the 1930s, was actually born in India. His parents were both missionaries. Bill, who was born in 1912, played alongside the Revd Christopher Tanner and the Revd Mervyn Hughes at Gloucester. Bill served as an army chaplain in the Second World War and was held as a prisoner of war from 1944 to 1945.

Sadly, Chris 'Kit' Tanner, who won 5 caps for England from 1930 to 1934, was killed in action during the Second World War. Posted to HMS *Fiji* as military chaplain, he was on board the ship when it was sunk in the Battle of Crete in 1941. Selflessly, he focused on saving other men before himself, repeatedly going back into the water to rescue others. He died minutes after being pulled out of the water for the final time. His incredible sacrifice earned him the posthumously awarded Albert Medal.

DERRICK MORGAN: IN HIS OWN WORDS

Winger Derrick Morgan played more than 280 games from 1983 to 1993, scoring over 160 tries.

My first glimpse of Kingsholm

'When I was 5 we moved from Swindon to Denmark Road in Gloucester. We moved on a Wednesday night and there must have been a game on because there was this incredible light in the sky. I remember thinking what the heck is that? As a kid I'd climb a lamppost to get into the ground and sit on the Tump, often with my lifelong friend Malcolm Preedy.'

Early heroes

'My heroes growing up were mostly French, like Sella or Blanco, or perhaps Welsh. I always wanted Wales to beat England as a kid because they played open, running rugby. England just tried to grind teams down with Dusty Hare kicking penalties.'

The Gloucester trials

'I first went to the trials in 1980/81 and I thought I'd done OK but because I never heard anything from Gloucester – I just went back to Longlevens. It was only when I went back a couple of years later that I realised the score. A few people said "where did you disappear to?" The trials were dog-eat-dog because everyone was fighting for a place. It was one of the biggest games of the season. There was a lot at stake and a lot of high tackles.'

The 48–6 cup final defeat to Bath in 1990

'We lost the league the week before and felt under pressure. You could feel it building up through the week. We went down by coach on the day of the match on the hottest day of the year. The air conditioning on the bus was not the best and we were stuck in traffic, wearing blazers, on a boiling hot coach. The boys were drained when we got there. We played well for 15–20 minutes but I think we'd have been better prepared if we had gone down the day before. I think they wanted us to treat it like it was just another game, but it wasn't.'

Breaking into the Gloucester team

'I was playing for the United side when Phil Pritchard broke his leg. They didn't realise he'd broken it at first so I filled in for him in the firsts and carried on playing for the United as well. I think I played versus Coventry on the Saturday, but all in all I played Saturday, Monday, Wednesday, Saturday and Monday.'

Gloucester's underrated backs

'I shared a room with the Leicester boys Barry Evans and Rory Underwood at an England under-23s trial and they said to me "It must be boring playing on the wing for Gloucester." I asked them how many tries they'd got that season and I think Rory said 10 and Barry 9. I said, "well I've got 25 and Nick Price on the other wing has got 30!" Gloucester always had a reputation for its forwards and we had a brilliant pack. But we had good backs too.

The best two centres I played with were Paul Taylor and Richard Mogg. Paul was very underrated. I remember once before we played Bath the press were going on about how Halliday and Guscott would cut Taylor and Mogg to ribbons. We kicked off and the ball came across the back line. Taylor hit Halliday and Mogg crunched into Guscott at the same time. We never saw either of them again. Paul and Moggy were proper centres. They would do their jobs and say to me and Nick Price "you score the tries". It was a team game.'

Rugby in general

'They say it's a different game nowadays but the principles should be the same. I was always taught to avoid contact. Sometimes I think modern players try to run through people with an "I'm bigger than you" mentality, when if they looked over their shoulder they'd see someone to pass to. Physicality has obviously improved but I'm not so sure ball skills and vision are as good. We've lost the ethos – it's about battering through now, although the best sides are different. Look at New Zealand, they're all ball-handlers.'

SCHOOLBOY STAR

Bill Hook, one of Gloucester's all-time great goal-kickers, made his debut for the club in 1938 while still a schoolboy at Sir Thomas Rich's. He was 17.

WHAT'S IN A NAME?

Various Gloucester players and the nicknames they are better known by:

Reggie	Tony Windo
Happy	Andrew Martin
Dougie	Trevor Woodman
Hambo	Mike Hamlin
Spanner	Dave Spencer
Zed	Olivier Azam
Kamo Kid	Ian Jones
Pog	Simon Amor
Jimmy	Hubert Boughton
Whacker	Charles Smith
The General	Mickey Booth
Django	James Forrester
The Jackal	Carlos Nieto
Dino	Bob Phillips
Shroom	Gareth Delve
Baggy	Brian Hudson
Pastie	Mark Cornwell

PETER ARNOLD ON DIGGER MORRIS

'I knew Digger very well. He was always telling stories and one of his favourites was how he joined the RAF before Christmas 1939. He volunteered, but only told his missus he wouldn't be home for Christmas. Well, he did get home for Christmas ... in 1945!

'Digger was a very hard man who told me he got his nickname because he liked to give people a little dig with his left hand. The true reason was that he worked for the council digging holes. He said his favourite game was against a "Kiwi outfit" in 1945. The Kiwi outfit was actually the All Blacks. He said he didn't remember much because he got dropped on his head in the first half, but he said the second half was all right!'

Peter Arnold has been involved with producing Gloucester RFC match programmes since 1975. The first Gloucester match he ever saw was in 1938 versus Harlequins. 'I actually supported Harlequins that day because I thought their kit was prettier,' he said.

WHERE ARE THEY NOW?

Steve Boyle appeared more than 300 times for Gloucester, won 3 England caps and played in two cup finals. He now owns the Pilgrim Hotel in Much Birch, Hereford.

12 ANGRY MEN

Gloucester defeated Moseley 17–6 in the inaugural RFU Challenge Shield final at Twickenham on 29 April 1972. It was a controversial game that saw Moseley's Nigel Horton sent off for punching Dick Smith following the second scrum after just 4 minutes.

Moseley finished the game with 12 men because of injuries to Tim Smith and Ian Pringle. Smith sustained a rib injury, while Pringle hurt his knee following a collision with Tom Palmer.

Gloucester fell behind to a Malcolm Swain try, converted by Sam Dobie. The sending-off of policeman Horton changed the complexion of the match and it wasn't long before winger John Dix hit back with an unconverted try. With Moseley down to 13 men, Roy Morris raced in for another unconverted score. Eric Stephens landed a penalty, while Mickey Booth and Tom Palmer both dropped goals.

Stephens claimed the match was an anti-climax after superb away wins at London Welsh and Coventry in previous rounds. He said: 'It was supposed to be a showcase final but it was a forwards battle in the pouring rain. It was a peculiar game, but Moseley took a risk with injured players. I must admit I enjoyed the semi-final with Coventry far more. It ended 6–6 and I kicked a penalty and a drop-goal that bounced over off the bar. Coventry thought we would have to replay at Gloucester. They didn't know the rules; but we did – we knew we were through on the away rule.

'That same year half of our side played in the team that won the County Championship by beating Warwickshire. It was like a re-run of that Coventry game because 14 of the 15 Warwickshire players came from Coventry. I played on the wing that day and had to mark David Duckham but we managed to keep him quiet.'

TOM PALMER: IN HIS OWN WORDS

The 1972 cup final win over Moseley

'The Moseley press were horrendous to us but the sending off of Horton was right. He hit Dick Smith right in front of the referee. It was a silly thing to do.

'It was the 40th anniversary of the game in 2012. I've got an old video of the match and I watched it recently. It was an awful game, absolutely terrible. It was the first cup final but can you believe there were no replacements? It was our full side versus 12 and we just won. I wouldn't show the video to people, although modern pundits ought to listen to it just for Bill McLaren's commentary.'

Playing for Cornwall versus Gloucestershire

'I played in a winning Cornwall team at Kingsholm in 1969 while I was a Gloucester player. I also remember losing to Gloucestershire at Camborne. I was up against Booth and

Hopson and recall Mickey Burton was about to punch me, thought about it for a split second and let me off.'

The modern game

'How more people don't get seriously injured I'll never know. I have to say I prefer to watch old games because defences are so on top now. We just turned up and played. I watch modern players warm up before a game and it looks quite a hard session. That would have been our training.'

Tom Palmer joined Gloucester in 1968 after moving to the area from Cornwall. He played more than 200 games from 1968 to 1974 and subsequently served on the Gloucester committee from 1974 to 1982. Not bad for someone who played football for Truro up to the age of 16. It was his neighbour, who was treasurer of Truro RFC, who persuaded him to give rugby a go. Tom played rugby for Truro from 1959 to 1966 and represented Cornwall against Australia, Fiji and the All Blacks. In retirement he splits his time between Gloucestershire and Tenerife.

NO ROOM AT THE INN

In 1974, Gloucester were blacklisted by a number of hotels when trying to find accommodation for their end of season tour of Devon and Cornwall.

JOHN WATKINS, THE PROP FORWARD

Now a respected referee, John Watkins played 386 games for Gloucester, captained them for three seasons and won seven caps for England. Today, he'd be among the best-paid players in the country, but he's glad he played in the amateur era.

'I wouldn't swap my time for a million pounds,' he said. 'I used to go to work on Saturday mornings before a game. Training was two nights per week at the club, although I used to do my own training on top of that.

'I was 13–14 stones in my prime. Nowadays I'd be too light to play on the wing, let alone the back-row!'

Curiously, Watkins took up rugby through table tennis. He regularly played ping-pong at the Gordon League club in Gloucester (often against Bill Dawe) but got roped into making the numbers up for the men's rugby teams on Saturdays from the age of 13. By the late 1960s Watkins had stepped up to Gloucester RFC, where Peter Ford tried to convert him into a prop forward.

Watkins played prop for Gloucester United in a handful of matches but it was not the position for him. He decided he was going to play in the back row or not at all after getting 'flying lessons in Penzance'. He got himself fitter and became a first XV regular. In 1972, when a lot of the best players in the land opted not to go on tour to South Africa, he got his international call-up.

He said: 'I played for England from 1972 to 1975. I remember being picked against New Zealand at Twickenham and they wanted me to play at the front of the line-out and stop Sid Going. That was a negative move really.

'We got hammered by the Welsh twice. I was also involved in seven or eight other internationals but replacements only got on for injured players in those days.'

The only rugby mementoes in John's house are a couple of scrapbooks and a signed, framed picture of the Gloucester team that won the John Player Cup in 1978.

John said: 'Back then the players picked the captain. They presented me with this picture and they'd all written messages, thanking me for my support. That meant a lot.'

John became a referee after retiring from playing, but says the toughest opponents he faced in his playing career were Ian Kirkpatrick, Dai Morris, Terry Cobner, Tom David and the South African Jan Ellis. He plays down any suggestion that he is a Gloucester great, saying there is only one true club legend.

'Tom Voyce is the only true rugby legend in Gloucester as far as I'm concerned,' he said. 'He had a tremendous personality and I got to know him well because he came to all the games. He liked a pint and was one of the lads. He was so humble, considering all he achieved.'

John says the highlight of his career was making so many great friendships. He added: 'I played for England and went on three tours with the Barbarians with some of the best players in the world, but I'm basically a shy bloke.'

ONE TRUE VOYCE

Tom Voyce is a genuine Gloucester legend in every sense of the word. He won 27 caps for England in the 1920s (26 as a wing forward and one on the wing) and was also selected to represent the British Isles on a tour to South Africa. He helped England win back-to-back Grand Slams and finished on the losing side for his country only three times.

When he retired from playing he went onto the Gloucester committee and served as club chairman from 1939 to 1947. He later became president. He died in 1980 at the age of 82 after giving 69 years of his life to his only club.

BIG CROWD FOR OUTSIDERS

In December 1949, 10,500 watched the England Probables versus Possibles match at Kingsholm, even though no Gloucester players were selected to play in the game.

SENIOR DEBUT ... AT 11!

Rock-hard centre John Bayliss played more than 400 games for Gloucester from 1960 to 1976, captaining them in 1972/73. He also played 60–80 times for the county.

Born in Tredworth in 1943, Bayliss was an early starter. He represented England Boys Club versus Wales at 14 and made his Gloucester United debut at 16. He was an old hand by then, having made his debut in men's rugby five years earlier. He explained: 'My uncle Jack Goddard was a centre with Fielding & Platt and I used to follow them. I went with them to play Beckenham Extras and the opposition was one short. They asked if we had any spare players and although I was only 11 I was used to playing in the park with kids older than me. It was agreed that I would play on the wing for Beckenham opposite my cousin, the theory being that he would go easy on me. The only trouble was they put me on the wrong wing and I ended up playing against a kid called Bubbles who was 6ft 2in tall. It was David versus Goliath!'

Bayliss developed fast, as shown by his rise into the England Boys Club squad. This was an under-18s team, but the young Tredworth boy was first selected at 14 and ended up captaining the side for two years. It meant that when he went along to Kingsholm, most had already heard of him.

He said: 'People ask me why I never played for Tredworth, my local side, and the answer I give is that they never asked me. I was playing in a very good Fielding & Platt team but in 1959/60 most of our side had to go off for National Service. The team was decimated so my dad told me it was pointless staying – I might as well join Gloucester. I went down in 1960/61 and there were so many good players, people like Reggie Chamberlain, Cyril Thomas, Roy Long and Peter Ford. They made me feel very welcome. I've often heard others say that they weren't made to feel welcome but I think that might be sour grapes from a few who didn't make the grade. How can you not feel welcome around the likes of Alan Brinn and the Fowkes? They're such lovely people.'

John made his first XV debut against Leicester at Kingsholm, aged 17. He was notified by a phone call from Peter Ford. Gloucester won the match and Bayliss played well for the first 40 minutes. All he can remember about the second half is that he was exhausted. 'I was 12 stones 4lbs dripping wet. I had a big heart but I was a bit light for the physical side of the game. Don't forget, we used to go into the rucks and mauls in those days.'

It wasn't long before Bayliss had beefed up to 14 stones. He also developed a reputation as a ferocious tackler. He said: 'Tackling is all about running lines and a big heart. You can't do much with 12 stones but tackling is really a mentality. Straight running and tackling were always my strengths. I liked to stamp my game on the opposition. I liked to see the whites of their eyes and think "I'm on top of you".'

In 1973 Bayliss suffered an appalling injury that almost ended his life. He broke his neck in a match against Loughborough and subsequently spent a month in traction and eight months in a protective jacket to his waist.

He said: 'My dad died at Christmas. I was still a bit low but I was club captain. I came back too early when I had flu and I was lacking fitness. A big centre straightened on me, I mistimed the tackle and my head hit his thigh.

'I broke the top three vertebrae and what they call the hangman's joint. It was pretty serious. I remember walking into the hospital and going over to speak to someone I knew. Sister Donoghue shouted "Mr Bayliss, sit down at once ... a sudden jolt and you'll die."'

Most assumed Bayliss would never set foot on a rugby field again, including the player himself. He said: 'I was 29 and ready to call it a day. Then Mike Poole from Newent Rugby Club rang me out of the blue and asked if I fancied a game.

'I went along but said I would only play outside half and I wouldn't tackle. Imagine that, trying not to make a tackle when you're away at Spartans!

'The following week I agreed to play again, but I'd had enough of outside half. I played in the centre against

Cinderford and enjoyed it. The next thing I knew, Gloucester United wanted me to play against Cinderford the following week because they were short of players. Again, I agreed. The following week I was picked for Gloucester versus Newport at Kingsholm.

'I honestly never intended coming back. Later on I tore a ligament in my neck against Cleve, which left me with a lasting problem.'

In his prime, Bayliss was offered the chance to play rugby league for Warrington but he turned it down. It was a tough decision. 'The signing-on fee would have bought me a house and the wages were £30 per week plus bonuses. With a job as well it would have come to about £70 per week. I would have liked to have tried the game but the economics didn't seem good enough to switch from one end of the country to the other.'

Bayliss still goes to watch Gloucester four or five times a season. His grandson, who was seriously ill with a brain tumour, is Gloucester mad. Bayliss said: 'The club are brilliant with him and look after him first-class. For me personally, it's nice to meet old friends but it's not really what I want to do. I'm president of Gordon League and I've done some coaching for the likes of Lydney, but I believe in looking forward, not back.'

MY PAL BAYLO MADE ME WINCE

No one got a better view of those thumping John Bayliss tackles than fellow centre Richard Jardine. The pair complemented each other perfectly, with Jardine providing the midfield guile and elegance.

'I would sometimes wince watching John tackle, especially as my tackling was nowhere near as strong,' said Richard. 'Even when we played in golden oldie matches much later on, John went in just the same. He was the biggest influence on my rugby career, along with Mike Nicholls who was just so passionate.'

Jardine was a class act. The policeman from Chipping Sodbury was invited along to Kingsholm by Ivor Jones, who was team secretary of the police team and also had links to Gloucester. Jardine made his debut for Gloucester United versus Bristol on 23 September 1967. He went on to play more than 300 times for the first XV, featuring in both the 1972 and 1978 cup campaigns (he missed the 1972 final because of injury). He played for the county 26 times and toured Romania with England B.

Nowadays, Richard has little involvement with rugby and hardly even watches it. He said: 'I'm not a very good spectator. It's particularly hard watching England. I get so frustrated.'

OH BROTHER!

At the end of the nineteenth and the beginning of the twentieth centuries, six Cook brothers, Jim, Harry, Albert, George, Charles and Dave all played for Gloucester. Around the same time seven brothers from the Hall family also turned out for Gloucester.

A GLANCE AT THE FIFTIES

In **1950/51** Charlie Crabtree was the club's leading try-scorer with 10. There were some very low scores during this season, including 0–0 draws with United Services, Portsmouth, Lydney and Bristol, 3–0 wins over Wasps and Stroud, a 3–3 draw with Harlequins and a 3–0 defeat to Cheltenham!

In **1951/52** Gloucester won 30 of 45 matches and 12,000 fans witnessed the 14–0 home success against Cardiff.

Charlie Crabtree was leading try-scorer again with 16, while both R. Hodge and H. Wells made 44 appearances.

Gloucester used a total of 40 players in the **1953/54** season, winning 31 of 42. However, they lost 9–6 at home to Cheltenham – Cheltenham's first win at Kingsholm for twenty-four years.

1954/55 was disappointing, with only 19 wins out of 41. The following season, the club managed just 12 points from 28 January through to 10 March. They lost 19–3 to the Army, drew 0–0 with Swansea, lost 19–6 to Northampton, had 3 games cancelled owing to frost and crashed 22–3 against the RAF.

International opposition started to come to England during this decade and the cherry and whites lost 10–6 to a Romanian Bucharest XV in **1956/57**, but beat Milan 23–9 in **1958/59**.

1959/60 was a decent season. Bob Smith led the way with 12 tries and Terry Hopson made 41 appearances out of 42 as the club won 13 matches in a row from 24 October to 2 January. There were wins against Coventry, Oxford University, Leicester, Moseley, Cambridge University, Aberavon, Bath, Neath, Bath again, Coventry, OMTS, UAU and London Scottish. The run ended with a 6–3 loss at Leicester.

JIM JARRETT: IN HIS OWN WORDS

My second-row partnership with Alan Brinn

'When I came to Gloucester from Pontypool I was a number eight, but Gloucester were short of second-rows so I did what I could for the team. I had a very good partnership with Alan, we were like two pieces of a jigsaw. Brinny liked packing left and I liked packing right. He jumped short, I jumped in the middle. He was very solid, I ran about the field a bit more. We were both, if I say so myself, good scrummagers.'

My best captains

'Two stood out head and shoulders above the rest. Clive Rowlands, from my time at Pontypool, and Mike Nicholls. Mike was just a tremendous motivator who led by example.'

My toughest opponent

'I played against some of the very best but the man who caused me the most trouble was someone who is not very well known, Derek Simpson of Coventry. Coventry were among the toughest English opponents I played against and Derek was an awkward so and so and very aggressive. He was a lay preacher, but he was the dirtiest lay preacher I ever encountered.'

My favourite current Gloucester players

'Although I spend a lot of time in Spain nowadays, I still follow Gloucester. I admire James Simpson-Daniel, Andy Hazell, who I used to coach, and Olly Morgan. Charlie Sharples is an immense talent who can go a long way.

'I like Alex Brown too. He's a very good all-round forward who does a lot of unseen work.'

DID YOU KNOW?

Jim Jarrett used to sing in a choir and would often belt out 'The Old Rugged Cross' to his team-mates after matches.

DOUBLE DEATHS

In 1925, Gloucester player Stan Bayliss died a week after dislocating his neck in a match against Old Blues at Kingsholm. The following season, vice-captain Sid Brown ruptured a kidney against Aberavon. He finished the game, but died the next day.

THE GREAT PETER FORD

Peter Ford thought his call up to the England ranks was a joke. He said: 'I was 31 when I was called up versus Wales in 1964 and I also played that year against France and Ireland, but I was at the end of my career by then. I played in the trials – and the year before for the Barbarians – but to be honest I thought it was a joke.'

Ford joined Gloucester in 1951 at the age of 19. He played once for the second XV against Bream before making his first XV debut against Stroud. He was a permanent fixture after that, going on to play more than 500 times and scoring 146 tries. Ford retired from playing in 1965 but remained a dedicated committee man and selector. Few men, if any, have given more to the club.

When the game became professional in the mid-1990s Ford was against many of the changes that subsequently followed. He said: 'Finances were tight in the 1970s and '80s but when things changed I had to accept it or walk away. I was against professionalism at the time. I played in an era where you didn't play to be paid. It was against everything I was brought up to believe. I didn't want monetary rewards to play for Gloucester. A lot of people of my era were entitled to claim expenses but didn't.'

DID YOU KNOW?

When Peter Ford was called up for his first England cap he had to go out and buy a pair of white shorts – because Gloucester's shorts were black!

CENTENARY CLASH

To mark the club's 100th year, a Gloucester XV took on and beat a star-studded international XV by 24–14 in the 1973/74 season with tries from Peter Butler (two), Bob Redwood, John Haines and Keith Richardson, plus two conversions from Butler the Boot.

Gloucester's team was: P. Butler, R. Clewes, T. Palmer, R. Jardine, R. Etheridge, R. Redwood, J. Spalding, K. Richardson, M. Nicholls, M. Burton, A. Brinn, J. Fidler, J. Watkins, J. Haines, D. Owen.

The international XV was: P. Villepreux (France), J. Janion (England), J. Dawes (Wales), J. Maso (France), D. Duckham (England), J. Berot (France), S. Smith (England), I. McLauchlan (Scotland), J. Young (Wales), A. Carmichael (Scotland), C. Spanghero (France), C. Ralston (England), N. MacEwan (Scotland), A. Neary (England), B. Dauga (France).

POTTER: THE NUMBER EIGHT WIZARD

When he first started playing for Gloucester, Mike Potter recognised very few of the opponents he was up against. 'I didn't know if they were internationals or not and I rarely ever read the match programmes,' he admitted.

'I'd look across at them and think "blimey, they've got some big blokes" but once you started playing it didn't matter. I got to know and recognise a few more people as I got older. I played against some excellent players, people like Gareth Edwards and Mervyn Davies.'

The blonde number eight played 220 times for Gloucester from 1968–74 after making his debut in a win over Lydney in 1968. He said: 'I was playing number eight for Coney Hill at the time and a relative of mine said to me at our dinner and dance "David Owen is packing it in at Gloucester, why don't you give it a go?"

'I played for the shirt and the city. I wasn't worried about England – if you were local, playing for Gloucester was like playing for England.'

Potter made his Coney Hill debut at 15. Growing up, he never went to Kingsholm to watch rugby. All that's changed and today he is a committed season ticket-holder. He said: 'Our biggest derbies were against Bristol. There was a big rivalry and some hard games with a lot of punch-ups. That was just part of the game. A bit like today, we didn't always do that well away from home, but at Kingsholm we were tough to beat. The crowds were not like they are now but they could give you a terrible time. I remember Roy Morris, our centre, getting a lot of stick. It was horrible.'

Potter says the Gloucester teams he played in were generally forwards-orientated, but he believes the club has been blessed with some tremendous kicking outside-halves over the years, such as Terry Hopson.

'You can't compare eras because we had to go to work, whereas the modern players are on the weights all the time,' he added. 'I worked for the council and my weights were loading and unloading bags of cement. Now they have ice baths after a game. We rubbed the bits that hurt and got on with it.

'I broke my shoulder against London Scottish but my worst injury was a punctured lung which I got playing for Coney Hill. I scored a try and received a kick in the ribs. In the old days we did a lot more drinking. We had some good tours to Devon and Cornwall – that was our end-of-season treat. After home games we got a barrel of beer but if you were too slow out of the showers it was all gone!'

BEATING LEICESTER IS SWEET

Defeating Leicester is always sweet but to do it in a prestigious Twickenham final is even more special. On 15 April 1978 Richard Mogg scored the try that gave Gloucester a narrow 6–3 John Player Cup final win over their arch rivals. The Tredworth winger burst through a couple of tackles just before half time, with Peter Butler adding an excellent touchline conversion.

Leicester and England kicker Dusty Hare struggled with his radar and was only able to slot home one of the many penalty opportunities that came his way. Not for the first time the Gloucester forwards bossed the game with Steve Mills striking against the head several times against England hooker Peter Wheeler. Mills played in a powerful front-row with Gordon Sargent and Mike Burton.

Man of the match, however, was Mogg, who also denied Leicester's Bob Barker a try late in the game with a memorable tackle.

Gloucester's starting XV in the final was: Peter Butler, Bob Clewes, Richard Jardine, Brian Vine, Richard Mogg, Chris Williams, Paul Howell, Mike Burton, Steve Mills, Gordon Sargent, Steve Boyle, John Fidler, John Watkins, John Simonett, Viv Wooley.

Their route to the final saw them beat Lydney 38–6 (home); Gosforth 19–10 (home); Wasps 13–3 (away) and Harlequins 12–6 (away).

WHERE ARE THEY NOW?

John Simonett, the forgotten man of Gloucester's 1978 cup-winning team, gave up rugby and a top teaching job for the world of magic and corporate speaking. John came to Gloucestershire to train as a PE teacher at St Paul's College in Cheltenham and played for Gloucester from 1976 to 1979.

The former schoolboy international and captain of British Colleges quit rugby at the age of 30 and then left his job as head of PE at King's School to make his living out of magic.

'My hobby got me out of teaching,' he said. 'I wasn't a star player but I played in a good era with the likes of Burton, Mills, Blakeway, Mogg and Kingston. Some fans remember me, often because I've got a funny name, but I'm usually the one from the 1978 team they forget.'

John now makes his living by giving after-dinner speeches, drawing on his phenomenal trained memory and his magic skills. He said: 'Some of the players used to pull my leg about the magic but I would often do tricks on the bus. I remember one game away at Gosforth, I entertained a dozen or so people in my room for around two hours.'

John still runs around with a rugby ball on Sunday mornings, turning out for a touch rugby team of 'old geezers' called The Dodderers.

BUMPS AND THE BOXING BOOTHS

Coalminer Adolphus Denzil Carpenter became the first player from the Forest of Dean to play for England when he took to the field against the South Africans in 1932. Born in 1900, Adolphus, better known as Bumps, played 336 times for Gloucester, scoring 7 tries. But for the Second World War, he would have captained Gloucester in 1939 at the age of 40.

Bumps spent most of his life working underground in Forest pits. After matches, he would go to the boxing booths to win clothes for his sons Denzil and George. He would also walk from Cinderford to Gloucester rather than spend his rugby expenses on bus fares.

Bumps only played once for his country, but he was named as an England reserve 28 times. He was picked to play against France in Paris, but in those days players had to pay their own expenses and Bumps couldn't afford to go. He did go on tour with the Barbarians though, to Wales!

When the Second World War broke out Bumps joined the RAF as a PT instructor, but was invalided out in 1942 after injuring his left arm. He returned to the pits but suffered serious damage to his skull in an underground accident in 1955 when some pipes clamped together and threw him hard against the pit roof. He never worked again, but led a happy retirement until his death in 1973.

Bumps started at prop against the Springboks in 1932 before switching to hooker in the second half. England won 7–0. Bumps brought home his England jersey as a souvenir. His wife Rose took the rose from the jersey and displayed it on the mantelpiece of their Cinderford home. The jersey still hangs in the Cinderford RFC clubhouse today.

DID YOU KNOW?

Many people believe Bumps Carpenter only won 1 England cap because he turned up for the post-match festivities wearing his miners' silk scarf. That, coupled with his background, was allegedly too much for the class-ridden authorities to bear.

Bumps continued to star for Gloucestershire at hooker, where he was propped by Bristol's Sam Tucker. Tucker was picked to play at hooker for England ahead of Carpenter.

CUP DRAW WON'T BE REPEATED

It seems strange that a cup final could go to extra time and still end without an outright winner, but that's exactly what happened in the 1982 John Player Cup final between Moseley and Gloucester.

Hooker Steve Mills captained a Gloucester side that gave their all, but they were more than matched by Derek Nutt's Moseley in a 12–12 Twickenham draw that saw the clubs share the cup.

Gloucester lost Mike Longstaff and Malcolm Preedy to injuries during the game, but they were fortunate to be able to call upon more than useful replacements in Paul Wood and Gordon Sargent.

Full-back Paul Ford, the son of Peter Ford, nudged Gloucester in front with two first-half penalties, but Moseley levelled the scores with two penalties from Mike Perry. Ford kicked his third penalty late in the game, but Perry responded to take the match into extra time. Perry dropped a goal for Moseley, but Ford struck back with a penalty off the posts.

'That season I played a lot of games but Peter Butler played in the semi-final,' recalled Ford. 'Peter Butler also played the week before the final but I was selected for the Moseley game. I suppose it caused a bit of controversy at the time.'

Ford went on: '1982 was one of Gloucester's better seasons. I remember cup final day was warm and there was a strong wind. There was a lot of kicking and it wasn't a particularly good game of rugby. The conditions probably suited Moseley more than us.

'That evening, after the game, we were meant to fly to South Africa so there was a lot going on. We only had a quiet celebration because we knew we were off.

'I hadn't played extra time before but we just got on with it. My last kick hit the post and went over which was a relief. I'd have got lynched if it hadn't!'

Gloucester's route to the final saw them beat High Wycombe 40–6 (home); Exeter 34–3 (home); Sale 13–6 (home) and Coventry 18–9 (away).

HOWELLER'S TOUGHEST OPPONENT

Paul Howell, one of the hardest scrum-halves ever to wear the Gloucester number 9 shirt, reckoned Terry Holmes was the toughest opponent he faced.

Howell was much more than just a scrum-half, he'd take the fight to the opposition like a back-row. He learnt his rugby at Lydney Secondary Modern School under John Fry.

He was firmly established in the Lydney first XV when he got the opportunity to play for Gloucester, following a serious injury to Peter Kingston. Kingston was out for the season with a knee injury so Howell agreed to play for Gloucester versus Cheltenham. The following week he played for Gloucester in a 6–3 loss against Gosforth in the John Player Cup.

Howell was part of Gloucester's successful John Player Cup winning squad in 1977/78. He spent three years at Kingsholm before joining Bristol – frustrated that he was getting sent to Wales on Wednesday evenings while Kingston was playing on Saturdays. He ousted Richard Harding for a while at Bristol, but returned to Gloucester in 1982, where he was mainly used as a centre. The following season Howell went back to Lydney, where he played until his retirement at the age of 39.

SWAPPING HALF-BACKS

When Gloucester played Lydney in 1975, all four half-backs on show were men who had served both clubs with distinction. Chris Williams and Peter Kingston represented Gloucester that day, with Ian Wilkins and Paul Howell up against them.

STEVE OJOMOH: IN HIS OWN WORDS

My funniest memories

'Dave Sims, our captain, went out to toss the coin at Bath and came steaming into the changing room to get us geed up. He said, "Boys, they've just called us Gloucester mutes." It went quiet for a bit then Deacs (Andy Deacon) piped up, "But we are Gloucester mutes."

'We played a lot of cards in my time at Gloucester. Richard Hill didn't mind as long as it was out in the open. I remember one card school getting a bit ridiculous and Rory Greenslade-Jones, a real character, lost a bit of money. A few days later there was a bit of a get-together and Ian Sanders was there with his wife. He said to Rory, "Do you like my wife's new dress and shoes? Thanks mate, you paid for that!"'

Joining Gloucester from rivals Bath

'I have very happy memories of my three-and-a-half years at Gloucester. The camaraderie was something else. Although I came from Bath, the Shed and the crowd embraced you if they could see you were giving your all for the cherry and white shirt.

Of course you had to win the players over and at the time if you won over Deacs you won over the rest. I remember him looking at me over his little glasses, trying to work me out when I first arrived.

'Everything he said to me was related to Bath. It wasn't "how's the flat Steve?", it was "how's that Bath flat?"

'Even now he still calls me Steve from Bath. It was all in fun but I knew what he meant. I wasn't just playing for the Gloucester shirt, I was defending the city.'

Richard Hill

'When I joined Gloucester in 1997, Richard Hill, who I played alongside at Bath, was coach. Richard was a tough coach, but he wouldn't ask you to do anything that he wouldn't do himself. He set high standards and found it frustrating that some of the players were not that professionally minded.

Richard was still learning and professionalism was new. There were lots of good pros like Simon Devereux who was a great trainer, but I wouldn't put myself in that class.'

The dressing room banter

'It was like being back at school. You had to be on your guard else someone would be wearing your clothes into the showers. The Welsh boys were the butt of most of the jokes. We weren't the most talented team I ever played in but the team spirit was something else. It was better than I had experienced at Bath. There was a great collectiveness.

'When Philippe Saint-André came in he built that up. He had money to spend and bringing in the likes of Ian Jones helped take things to the next level.'

Steve Ojomoh now runs his own children's nursery – in Bath!

PROPER OLD BOYS

What do the following have in common? Well, they all played for Gloucester Old Boys: John A'Bear, Andy Hazell, Bill Hook, Digger Morris, Paul Ford, John Brain, Paul Knight, Paul Mansell, Bob Timms, Kevin Dunn, John and Viv Wooley, Dai Gent, John Gadd, Steve Baker, Francis Edwards, Nigel Smart, Roy Long and Tommy Burns. The Old Boys, who were formed in 1904, have produced four full internationals, Dai Gent, F.G. Edwards, Bill Hook and Andy Hazell.

NIGHT SHIFTS ON THE BEAT

When he first started out with Gloucester, Ron Etheridge worked as an engineer. He changed direction by joining the police force – something team-mate and fellow policeman Jerry Herniman advised him not to do as it would affect his rugby.

'He was right,' admitted Ron. 'My game did suffer, for a while at least. Gloucester had a lot of people in the police force but they didn't all do shift work like me. I did shifts in Cheltenham. I can remember coming straight back from a game at Harlequins with Peter Ford because I had to go to work.'

Born on the Isle of Bute in 1951, Ron Etheridge was a running full-back who didn't kick goals. A Scottish trialist, he played more than 180 times for Gloucester, scoring 40 tries. Ron's Gloucester career spanned three decades, from 1969 to 1980. He made his first XV debut against Coventry after just 2 games for the United side, away at Newbury and away at Bath.

He said: 'I had a fantastic time and the centenary season was the best because we had a good team and there was a lot going on. The strength in depth throughout the county was incredible.'

Ron says Gloucester's physicality shocked him at first. 'I remember a fracas against Coventry. John Watkins came back from talking to the ref and said "look out Ron, it's all going to kick off."

'Our forwards were so ferocious, nobody liked playing us. We had good backs but other sides didn't like our physicality.'

THE MAN WHO NEVER RETIRED

Peter Kingston never officially retired from playing for Gloucester. The England scrum-half slipped into the United side, gradually taking on more of a coaching role. At the age of 41 he found himself on the Gloucester bench against Sale, but was relieved not to get on. At the end of his career he even had a few games for Pontypool, after being persuaded to do so by Eddie Butler.

Kingston first joined Gloucester in 1974 after a couple of seasons with Moseley (he had a teaching job in Birmingham).

The prime reason for his switch was the fact that he had landed a new teaching job in Swindon.

Kingston made his Gloucester debut in a midweek game against the Italian side L'Aquila, keeping his place for the following Saturday's game versus Coventry. He quickly ousted John Spalding from the number 9 shirt and in 1975 was picked for England's tour of Australia. He was only 23 and surprised to be selected. England played well in the First Test in Sydney, but lost 16–9.

That match was rough, but the Second Test was a veritable bloodbath that became known as the Battle of Ballymore. Kingston's Gloucester team-mate Mike Burton became the first English player ever to be sent off as England lost 30–21.

Kingston, like many others who made that trip, slipped ignominiously back into club rugby after the tour. He sustained a serious knee ligament injury in 1977 and it was two years before he won his England place back. He played three times in the 1979 Five Nations under the captaincy of Bill Beaumont, including a 7–6 win over France. It was the only time he played in a winning England side. His last game for England was the 27–3 hammering against Wales in Cardiff.

There was a tour to the Far East soon after that and Kingston wasn't selected. Steve Smith replaced him and helped England to win the Grand Slam in 1980.

Now semi-retired, Kingston still coaches the under-14s team at Pates Grammar School.

PETER KINGSTON: IN HIS OWN WORDS

Life at Kingsholm

'The Gloucester side I joined was up there with the best – all the Welsh sides said we were the toughest English side. Playing scrum-half behind a Gloucester pack in those days was an armchair ride. I grew up in Lydney but as a boy I would often catch the train up to Kingsholm to watch games. I aspired to play there and still regard it as a privilege that I did.'

Being dropped

'I was unlucky to be on the bench for two cup finals. In 1978 Paul Howell was preferred to me and I also missed out on the 1982 final, I think it was Steve Baker who was selected at scrum-half. Nowadays they have rotas, but it wasn't like that. The team played 50-plus games per season and you wanted to play them all. If you didn't play you weren't rested, you were dropped.'

Training

'Ivor Oakes would take training in his hobnail boots after a day on the building site. It was hardly scientific, but it was hard. If we had a bad loss on the Saturday we got a beasting as a punishment. Before games we used to do running on the spot in the dressing room. I can actually remember the first time we went out to warm up on the pitch before a game – Mickey Burton was captain and it was at Bedford. We lost by 30–40 points. Burton was a good trainer but that seemed revolutionary at the time.'

The 1975 England tour to Australia

'It was a tough tour all round. Australia weren't supposed to be that strong; they were more known for their Aussie Rules and Rugby League in the 1970s. I went with Blakeway and Butler and it was an experimental squad. I played in both Tests – we just lost in Sydney, then it was the Battle of Ballymore, Burton's game. All the matches were tough, playing New South Wales felt like a Test match.

'Looking back, I think the balance of selection was probably wrong but the England selectors were always chopping and changing – there was no continuity. I suppose the big difference was that there were lots of players to pick from. Nowadays, there are only half a dozen or so English scrum-halves playing in the Premiership.'

Watkins the governor
'John Watkins was fantastic, a real head-first player. He was so brave, he was always having stitches. He was the Lewis Moody of his day but a better player.'

Local boys
'Local boys now are probably as good as ever but clubs no longer have the time to bring people on. If things are not going right they need a quick fix so they go out and buy players. It's all about getting points on a Saturday and avoiding relegation. Sometimes I see faces at Kingsholm, young blokes in the crowd, and I think to myself "why aren't you playing?" ... There's plenty of time to watch after your mid-30s and 40s. It's much better to play.'

Size matters
'I was only 5ft 8in tall and 10½ stone when I played, the same weight as I am now. Today's centres are bigger than a lot of the second-rows from my era. Players might be bigger and fitter but we played with every bit as much commitment as they do now. We played our guts out.'

Chris Williams
'Chris was probably the best 10 I played with. He got 1 cap in Paris and deserved more.'

Coaching England Schools
'I coached the England Schools team for eight years and the 1997 side was arguably the best England schools side ever. We had Tindall, Wilkinson, Simon Danielli, Balshaw, Sheridan, Borthwick, Flatman and Mears. We went on a six-week tour of Australia and it was obvious some of those boys were special.'

DID YOU KNOW?

Scrum-half Peter Kingston played alongside outside half Chris Williams for six different teams: Lydney Grammar School, England Schools, Lydney, St Paul's College (Cheltenham), Gloucester and Gloucestershire.

BURTON'S ONLY
ENGLAND TRY

Mike Burton's sending-off against Australia in 1975 didn't end his tour. He escaped a ban and was drafted in to play against a Queensland XV in Townsville where he scored his only try for England. He celebrated like he'd scored the winning touchdown in a World Cup final!

TAYLOR'S ONE-LINERS

Paul Taylor knew how to make his team-mates laugh. Captaining Gloucester in a tense cup semi-final against Bath, he attempted to deliver the killer team-talk. However, his team-mates could only fall about laughing when he demanded '80 per cent for the whole 100 minutes'.

On another occasion, Dave Spencer attempted to tackle legendary New Zealand second-row hard-nut Andy Haden, but succeeded only in ripping his boot off.

'What do I do with it?' enquired Spencer.

'Give it him back, for God's sake!' replied Taylor.

PLAY-OFF SYSTEM NOT FAIR

Gloucester have finished top of the Premiership three times in the modern era, but have never won a Championship final.

In 2002/03, the club finished 15 points ahead of runners-up Wasps in the table having impressively won 17 and drawn two of their 22 games. Their only defeats were away at London Wasps, Leicester Tigers and Leeds Tykes. However, a three-week break at the end of the season worked against them and they lost the Twickenham final 39–3 in front of a crowd of 42,000, Ludovic Mercier kicked a 4th-minute penalty for Gloucester, but Wasps ran in 3 tries through Josh Lewsey (2) and Joe Worsley, with Alex King adding 24 points with the boot.

In 2006/07 Gloucester finished level at the top of the league standings with Leicester Tigers, having won 15 of their 22 games. They trounced Saracens 50–9 at Kingsholm in the play-off semi-final to set up a winner-takes-all showdown with Leicester at Twickenham. A crowd of 59,400 saw the Tigers win that game 44–16. Ryan Lamb scored Gloucester's only try with Willie Walker kicking three penalties and a conversion.

The following season, 2007/08, Gloucester topped the table again. They finished on 74 points, 4 more than second-placed Wasps. Huge disappointment followed with a 26–25 defeat to Leicester Tigers in the play-off semi-final at Kingsholm in front of 16,500 fans. Gloucester had led 12–3 at half time through four Ryan Lamb penalties. James Simpson-Daniel went over for a try after the break, with Lamb converting and slotting another penalty.

Leicester stayed in the game with tries from Alesana Tuilagi and Aaron Mauger, plus two conversions and three penalties from Andy Goode. Willie Walker put Gloucester in front with a drop-goal 5 minutes from time, but Andy Goode broke the home fans' hearts with a 78th-minute drop-goal of his own to ensure his side became the first team ever to win a play-off semi-final away from home.

MILK CAME FIRST

Adey Powles didn't take up rugby until he was 19 because he refused to give up his milk round on Saturday mornings. This meant that, until he was 19, the only competitive rugby he played was for the Rising Sun's pub team in Broadwell.

Powles started playing seriously for Berry Hill before switching to Gloucester following a short stint at Worcester. He played under Barry Corless, Viv Wooley and Richard Hill, but his Gloucester career flourished when Philippe Saint-André took over.

He became a crowd favourite and Saint-André even arranged for him to represent the French Barbarians against Wales in the first game at the Millennium Stadium in Cardiff with the roof shut. Sadly, at the age of 33, a terrible car crash left him with serious neck injuries and ended his career overnight.

SAVED BY THE RFU

Three Gloucester players were originally booked on the ill-fated Turkish Airlines DC 10 which crashed in Paris in 1974, killing everyone on board. Mike Burton, John Watkins and Peter Ford were among those switched to a Pakistani Airlines plane on the instruction of RFU officials, who wanted to keep the England party together.

LLOYD GARDINER'S HEROES

'Paul Howell was always one of my favourites, and outside half Les Jones. It was nice to play behind a pack of forwards like Gadd and Teague. It was certainly different to playing at Spartans. I've always enjoyed playing alongside my mate Bobby Fowke too, because we grew up together.

'One of the 10s I enjoyed playing with most was Mike Hamlin, a good leader, who was calm and kicked well. He was just a good all-round player.

'Playing for Gloucester was brilliant. We used to live over the back of the ground and I'd climb over the fence for training. When I was a kid I was a ball boy and sold programmes, all for free. We used to play our own games on the Tump while the main game was going on.'

Lloyd Gardiner played for Gloucester from 1988 to 1992.

MR GLOUCESTER LOVES PARIS IN THE SPRING

Arthur Hudson scored 9 tries for England in 8 appearances and, incredibly, all of those tries came on just two grounds. He scored three international tries on the Athletic Ground in Richmond, and six at the Parc Des Princes Stadium in Paris – including four in one match in the 35–8 win over the French in the 1906 Home Nations.

Hudson made his England debut in that 1906 season at the age of 24, scoring on debut versus Wales. He scored two more tries in Paris against the French in his last appearance for England in March 1910.

Hudson captained Gloucester from 1906 to 1908 and served on the committee in a number of roles. He died in July 1973, at the age of 90. Arthur's son Gordon followed him into the Gloucester team, but reached his peak during the Second World War. It probably robbed him of the chance to win England caps, but he still emulated his father by scoring four tries in an international match. Serving as a corporal in the RAF, Gordon scored 4 tries in a wartime services international between England and Wales in March 1943.

MERIT MEN

Gloucester won the John Smith's Merit Table in 1985/86, losing only 1 of their 9 games, to Harlequins. They scored 1,015 points with 286 from Tim Smith. Derrick Morgan scored 27 tries and Jim Breeze 17.

BREEZE MOVED LIKE THE WIND

Not many wingers make the step-up to top level club rugby at the age of 26 or 27 and go on to play more than 200 games. Jim Breeze did exactly that.

He was Gloucester's top seasonal try-scorer twice in a career that ran from 1984 to 1990. Prior to joining Gloucester, he played for All Blues and Stroud. Breeze always had a soft spot for Gloucester, having been a ball boy at Kingsholm for many years.

He said: 'I played for All Blues from the age of 16 before joining Stroud. I played 140-plus games for Stroud and, to be totally honest, had no real urge to go to Gloucester. You've got to remember that the Stroud side back then was extremely strong. We beat Gloucester, Bath and Bristol one year.

'Mike Teague, who I started out with at All Blues, kept onto me to give Gloucester a go so eventually I agreed, once Stroud had been knocked out of the John Player Cup. I didn't have to wait long to get in the first XV because Nick Price picked up a serious injury.'

Breeze says standing behind some formidable Gloucester packs was always special, and it was a particular privilege to watch the back-row at work.

'It was usually Gadd, Teague and either Dave Spencer or Mike Longstaff and they took no liberties,' he recalled. 'John Gadd is a lovely quiet man, but he changed when he got the smell of liniment in his nostrils. He became our enforcer. He never stayed down.

'When Teaguey first got picked for England it was as a blindside flanker, John's position, and I think he felt a bit embarrassed because he was best mates with Gaddy. I think he rang him up and said "this cap should be yours".'

Breeze was a Merit Table winner with Gloucester in 1985/86 but doesn't rate it as a big deal. He said: 'It was a strange competition because it was decided on averages. You could play 4 games and win the league, while everyone else played 10. When I started, the cup was definitely the priority but by the end of my time the club was starting to take the leagues much more seriously.'

Gentleman Jim rates Rory Underwood and David Trick as two of the toughest opponents he faced. He still has the odd run-out for the Cherry Pickers but because he works most Saturdays (he owns the Motor House car business near Stroud), he rarely goes back to his old stamping ground.

He said: 'I got nothing for playing the game, in fact it was only in my last couple of seasons that I got £10 for boots. Until then, I bought my own boots and training kit. It was totally amateur but it was an honour to play for Gloucester. I see players now jumping from club to club but most people who finished at Gloucester in my day gave up the game, because they didn't want to play anywhere else.

'The leagues have done a lot for rugby but they have not helped loyalty.

'I'm the other side of 50 now and it hurts. I'm well-known in this area but it's a long time since I played – more than twenty years. It's all in the past. But rugby circles are special – I can go to any bar in the world and start a conversation about the game. I don't usually say "I've played for Gloucester", I just say, "I've played a bit".'

THE PURCHASE OF CASTLE GRIM

Gloucester's ground is often referred to as Castle Grim, but why? The answer has nothing to do with what opponents think about their chances of winning a game at Kingsholm! The club's ground was actually built on an area of land that used to be known as the Castle Grim Estate in Dean's Walk. The land belonged to the Ecclesiastical Commissioners, but the lease was held by Mr A.V. Hatton, who also had an option to buy it. Mr Hatton offered the club 7 acres of land for around £4,400. However, the Castle Grim land was not the only option on the table.

There was also an opportunity to buy a field in Sheephouse Road belonging to Mr H.J. Cullis, as well as a site in Bristol Road, next to Ashbee's Mill.

At a general meeting at the Northgate Assembly Rooms, many favoured the Sheephouse Road option, which was actually cheaper, but some feared attendances would fall dramatically if they took this move (the land was about three-quarters of a mile from the Wagon Works). Some of those favouring the Castle Grim option pointed to the fact that the site could be utilised as an athletic ground, which could be used to generate income through the summer. The site also included a number of houses and a builders' yard, which brought in a rental of £39 per year.

Eventually a resolution was put forward by Mr Bennett and seconded by Mr Phillips that 'this meeting is strongly in favour of acquiring, on the best terms possible, the Kingsholm site as an athletic ground'.

The resolution was carried by an overwhelming majority and by the end of that fateful night in 1891 small shareholders had already pledged a total of £750. The club sought to raise the cash needed to buy the site with a mortgage of £3,000 and a limited liability company offering shares at £1.

DICK SMITH:
A MAN FOR ALL OCCASIONS

Flanker Dick Smith served Gloucester from 1958 to 1976 as a player, scoring more than 100 tries. He subsequently moved into a coaching role and was in charge of the team that won the 1982 John Player Cup final.

Born in Brockworth in 1940, Dick was educated at Crypt School and originally played for Old Cryptians. His Gloucester debut came against Neath in 1958, playing in the centre. He captained Gloucester in 1968/69 and 1969/70. His first year as skipper was particularly successful, producing 32 wins with a record 882 points scored.

He said: 'The captains used to do everything but we had three wise men in Dr Alcock, Tom Voyce and Arthur Hudson. They were terrific people. Dr Alcock, a surgeon, would come into the dressing room after matches to make sure you were OK. Cyril Thomas was my first captain and he was also a big influence.'

Dick says the best players he played with were Terry Hopson, Mickey Booth, Bill Paterson, who joined from Sale for a couple of seasons, and full-back Tony Lewis.

He also says what he achieved as a coach gave him far more satisfaction than anything he did as a player.

'In 1981 we only lost 3 games all season with a team of nobodies. Of course, they weren't nobodies but they were unknown players just starting to come through, like Orwin, Gadd and Longstaff. Watching my son Ian play for Scotland and captain Gloucester also gave me a lot of pride. In my day it wasn't viable to go up to Scotland although the question about me playing for them did come up. They said I wasn't eligible because I played in about a dozen trials for England. People forget Ian also played for England A.

'I think I was worth a cap. When England were preparing to tour South Africa I was training with them in London. On the day of departure, the hotel was surrounded by anti-apartheid protestors. We had to get on a bus and leave our cars behind.

We were taken through the back gate at Heathrow and had to watch those going on tour make their way onto the plane. Then we went back to our cars.'

Dick played representative rugby for the Barbarians and remembers having a heavy night after a Monday night game versus Swansea. The Barbarians had another game against Newport on the Tuesday, but Dick wasn't playing. Well, not until Roger Quinnell got the kick-off time wrong and failed to turn up on time.

'I was sat in the stand when I got waved down to play,' he said. 'Roger Lane of Cardiff was the other wing forward. Someone had to play in the second-row so I said I'd do it because I was still the worse for wear!'

Dick's grandson Sam has represented the Gloucester A team and he'd love to see a third generation of Smiths running out at Kingsholm. It might tempt him back to his old stamping ground, because nowadays he's not a great rugby watcher. 'Rugby used to be a game for all shapes and sizes but I'm not sure it is anymore. I can't understand the game now, with men with the ball at the back of a ruck. To me, the five or six in front of them trundling down the pitch are all offside. The rolling maul is killing the game. Put the ball on the floor and make a ruck. I watch a bit of rugby on TV but I don't go much. I prefer golf.'

Dick is one of an elite band of five to have played 500 games for Gloucester. He laughs as he recalls what he was presented with for such an achievement. 'I got a little clock made of plastic presented to me in the dressing room. It was very low-key. I've still got the clock, but I'm not sure it works. I'm not sure it ever did!'

JAILED FOR NINE MONTHS

In 1996, 27-year-old Gloucester forward Simon Devereux was jailed for nine months when a jury at Kingston Crown Court found him guilty of inflicting GBH with intent on Rosslyn Park's Jamie Cowie. Devereux lashed out after the referee blew for a penalty after a ruck, breaking Cowie's jaw in three places.

DID YOU KNOW?

Former winger Tom Beim went on to become one of the country's leading polo players. What does Tom have in common with Darren O'Leary? They both scored five tries in a single European match. Tom's five came against Roma in the Heineken Cup in October 2000, while Darren touched down five times against Gran Parma in the European Shield in 2002.

ETHERIDGE SWITCHES ALLEGIANCE

John Etheridge represented England B while a Gloucester player, but after joining Northampton in 1990/91 he became Irish, going on tour with the Emerald Isle to New Zealand. In 1992/93 he played for Ireland B versus England B, where he was up against Kevin Dunn, a team-mate four years before.

WHERE ARE THEY NOW?

New Zealander Robert Todd, who represented Gloucester from 2001 to 2004, is a rugby coach at Canford School. Todd left Gloucester for Sale but retired with immediate effect in 2006 after being diagnosed with a potentially fatal skin cancer. Following extensive treatment, Todd is cancer-free and studying to become a chiropractor.

DID YOU KNOW?

Arnold Alcock, a key administrator who was club president for forty-five years, was nicknamed Doc because he was a leading surgeon at Gloucestershire Royal Hospital.

PONTYPOOL: LIKE A SCENE OUT OF *GLADIATOR*

Builder Tim Smith is one of Gloucester's top all-time points-scorers after an illustrious thirteen-year career at Kingsholm. Smith joined Gloucester from Gordon League, where he finally settled on playing at full-back.

He almost gave up the game though, after getting badly stamped on at the age of 16. He said: 'I played mostly at outside half or in the centre as a youngster but Gordon League wanted to play me on the wing. In one particular game the rain was hammering down, it was freezing cold and I never touched the ball once so I said "I'm not playing there again". I only had 3 or 4 games at full-back when Brian Russell said "I think you'd better get yourself down to Kingsholm".'

Tim went along to Gloucester around the same time as Ian Smith, Pete Jones, Andrew Stanley, Steve Artus and his pal Cormac O'Donoghue. In the notorious Yellows versus Reds trial match, Tim and Cormac attempted to wow those watching with a move they had devised at Gordon League, but it didn't come off. It resulted in the opposition scoring a try and an almighty rollocking from their captain, Mike Longstaff.

There were plenty of highs and lows in Smith's career. He said: 'Losing 48–6 to Bath in the cup final was pretty bad. I was sat in the changing room afterwards and Teaguey could see I was down. He sat by me, gave me a beer and said "look, we were beaten by a better side. Chin up and move on."

'I also remember missing a kick from in front of the posts to beat Llanelli, who we hadn't played in years. It finished 7–7.

'I always enjoyed the Easter programme when you would play Saturday, Sunday and Monday against the likes of Broughton Park and Birkenhead and there would be 50–60 points scored. And the cup games, particularly the ones against Bristol. I enjoyed going to Cardiff and beating them for the first time in fifty years.

'On Wednesday nights the world and his mates would always drop out and that happened when we went to Pontypool one night to play the Wales pack plus David Bishop. We were 20-odd points down at half time but in the second half the Lord, Nick Price, scored a hat-trick and we won.

'When you went to Pontypool you'd think to yourself "where's the crowd?" Then they'd suddenly appear from the mountains like that scene from the film *Gladiator*, shouting "Pooler! Pooler!"'

Playing in the amateur era, Smith says he often handled pre-match nerves on a Friday night by going out on the town 'for a few ciders'. He said: 'On a Saturday, if we were playing at home, I'd walk to the ground with Derrick Morgan, who lived around the corner from me. We'd have our kit bags in hand. As you approached Brunswick Road you'd start to feel it. By King's Walk and Worcester Street the hairs on the back of your neck would be standing up. Even now, just talking about it, it brings it all back.'

Smith says Mike Teague, John Gadd, Phil Blakeway and Richard Mogg were the best players he played with. 'Teaguey and John Gadd were outstanding, you would scratch your head at some of the things John did. I remember Ian Milne, the Harlequins prop, going on about what he was going to do to Phil Blakeway, but Phil tore him apart. Phil wasn't a big man but you didn't mess with him. And he was surprisingly quick. I remember him catching Clive Dyke once in training. Moggy was a local boy who kept himself to himself. He didn't mix much with the opposition – it was Gloucester boys or nothing. Mike Slemen was around about the same time as him, but I always thought Moggy was the better player.'

Tim Smith still turns out for Gordon League's second XV. He said: 'They asked me to play for the firsts last season and I said no. When they asked why not I said "Because I'm nearly 50. I'm hardly the future."'

AND THE BAND PLAYED ON

Prior to the public address system being put in during the 1950s, Gloucester crowds were often entertained before the kick-off by the Cinderford Town Band.

RECORD-BREAKER BRINN

No man is ever likely to break Alan Brinn's amazing record of 572 appearances for Gloucester's first XV. Brinn joined his local club Hereford straight out of school but came to prominence when Hereford played an Invitation XV to mark the opening of their new clubhouse.

He said: 'I played against John Currie, the England second-row, and had a good game. A few people said to me that

I ought to step up, so my father took me to Gloucester for a trial because they were the nearest big club to me.'

Brinn says there was nobody to mentor him or show him the ropes at Kingsholm. It was sink or swim. 'You had to fend for yourself,' he said. 'The structure of the club was very different to today.'

Brinn played 3 times for England and made his international debut in 1972 – the same year as Gloucester's inaugural RFU Challenge Shield success. Like many of his peers, he rates the quarter-final cup victory at London Welsh that year as the best win of his career, even though it was a match he did not play in.

He said: 'The cup draws kept sending us away and I couldn't play against London Welsh because I'd been away with the England squad and hurt my knee. Jim Jarrett and Nigel Jackson played in the second-row that day.

'I was more nervous watching from the sidelines than if I had been playing. Don't forget, London Welsh in the early 1970s were like the Welsh national team and full of British Lions. No one gave us a chance, but we beat them.'

After retiring from rugby, Brinn served as Gloucester's chairman and was also an associate national selector.

PERCY'S POINTS

In 1898, Percy Stout scored 4 tries and kicked 5 conversions, two penalties and a drop-goal in a match against Weston-super-Mare. Percy won 5 caps for England and later became a stockbroker in Cairo. He was awarded the DSO in the First World War. His brother Frank captained England versus Wales in 1904 and won the Military Cross in the same conflict.

OH MICKEY YOU'RE SO FINE

Most who played alongside him cannot believe that Mickey Booth never won an England cap. England's loss was certainly Gloucester's gain as the man they called The General (after General Booth, the founder of the Salvation Army) played 471 times for the city club after making his debut in 1956 at the age of 17 against Oxford University.

Booth was a founder member of Longlevens RFC. He played for them for a single season and had a season and a bit with Spartans, before opting to try his luck at Kingsholm. He played three times for Gloucester United – against Cardiff University, the Royal Agricultural College and the Bristol Aircraft Company – before being elevated into the first XV. He captained Gloucester in 1962/63, 1964/65 and 1965/66.

Ironically, his last ever game for Gloucester's first XV was the 1972 cup final against Moseley, although he never planned his retirement.

He said: 'I had 16 seasons and loved every minute, but I just drifted away. The great Tom Voyce put me up for the committee and I served on that until the pro era. I was elected a life member and still go to all the games. It's a great privilege.'

Booth was a mercurial scrum-half with a box of tricks all of his own. He was a livewire who made things happen. He was also a keen student of the game who says he learned plenty from Don Rutherford.

'Don was ahead of his time and opened the game up for me. Training before Don was basically touch rugby, though Terry Hopson and I might throw a few passes to each other.

'It seems incredible now but I used to do the line-out signals by positioning my feet at the chap I wanted to catch the ball. It was hardly camouflage! Don was very clever. He was amazed at what we were when he joined us. He said to me "you're a very good kicker out of hand but do you realise you give possession away?" He got me to kick correctly in order to gain possession again, high enough but not too deep. He got me to tell my winger to come out flat or to get John Bayliss running through for the grubber.'

Booth says the other big influences on him in his early days at Gloucester were Jack and Roy Fowke and hooker Cyril Thomas, who he dubbed 'technically incredible'.

'It peeves me to see the way the ball is put into the set scrum now,' he said.

'I lost so many games at the last scrum of the match because the ref said I put the ball in crooked. It's a different game now but some of the changes I am in favour of, such as lifting in the line-out. You get a much cleaner ball.'

Mickey is not bitter that he did not get an England cap, adding: 'In those days there were only four internationals a season and three England trials. Now there are more games but no trials. So many players get 1 or 2 caps because I think they give you a game to see if you're good enough.'

Booth was famous for feigning to run away from the back of scrums without the ball. He said: 'I'm more ashamed of it now, what skill is there in running away without the ball? It was an off-the-cuff thing, but I think we were more inventive than we were given credit for. People said we played nine–man rugby but we had some very good backs such as Bayliss, Clewes and Hopson. The London teams were not as gritty as they are now and found us a bit robust.'

Booth recently went past the Aberavon ground on a coach trip and could not believe how peaceful it looked. He turned to his friend and said 'there are a few litres of my blood and some of my teeth out there!'

'We used to go to Aberavon by train and when we got off at the station we'd walk to the ground and have to help the kit man carry the kit. We used to go to London by train, too. We had to be at the station on time. When we got off we'd go to the buffet bar for roast beef, Yorkshire pudding, apple pie and custard, before getting a coach to the ground.

'They were different times. I remember they used to lay out thirty pieces of 1-inch bandage before the games for your tie-ups and if one snapped you didn't get another. The man who looked after the baths would cut pieces of carbolic soap like Oxo cubes and he'd only put fifteen out. They were happy days. It was an honour to play for Gloucester. We used to change by the clock and when we ran out we'd see the cathedral and think that's our city. Now it's an honour to wear the players' tie and blazer.'

MIKE NICHOLLS RIDES A WHITE HORSE AND THE GENERAL DOES A DEL BOY

Jim Jarrett says two of the funniest moments he can remember from his time at Gloucester happened on the same evening, returning from an away game at Coventry.

He said: 'We had a very good night and when we called back at Kenilworth Rugby Club we'd already had quite a few drinks. It was a very cold night and there was a white frost. In a field next to the club there was a white horse with steam coming out of his nostrils and Mike Nicholls said "I'm going to ride him". We gave him a hand up and he got on but when we looked up he'd kicked his legs in the air and sent Mike flying.

'Inside the club we were at the bar where Mickey Booth did the original *Only Fools and Horses* fall. At the side of the bar was a door and Mickey leant against it. We saw both soles of his feet shoot up into the air and he disappeared into the cellar. He came up looking like Norman Wisdom at his worst!'

Jim added: 'In our era rugby was a very social thing. We stopped everywhere and stayed out as a team. If you went home there had to be an emergency. We drank with the opposition and stayed in their clubhouses. There were no friends on the field – that was especially true to us – but after the game it was totally different. We made some very good pals.'

MASTER TACTICIAN AHEAD OF HIS TIME

Don Rutherford was awarded the OBE for services to rugby in 2000. Rutherford, who won 14 caps for England, was the RFU's first ever technical director of rugby. In thirty years at the RFU he also served as director of rugby, helping to develop many of the nationwide structures that exist today.

TAKE IT WITH A PINCH OF SALT

Gloucester shared the Spa ground with the city's cricket club (the official tenants) until 1890/91 when they were given notice to quit. Attempting to thaw out the ground for a game with Swansea, officials used too much salt, which ruined the grass.

The club had previously been ordered to quit after the floodlights failed for a match against Rockleaze – resulting in some unruly behaviour from supporters. However, the council relented on this occasion when a petition was presented with 3,000 signatures.

Home subsequently became Kingsholm, then known as the Castle Grim Estate in Dean's Walk. A pitch was hastily prepared and the Kingsholm ground was officially opened on 10 October 1891.

LEADING FROM THE FRONT

Alfred Wadley, who captained Gloucester from 1932 to 1935, figured in every match of the 1935/36 and 1936/37 seasons.

DAVE SIMS – THE FIRST PROFESSIONAL

He became Gloucester's first ever full-time professional in May 1996 but Dave Sims still feels unhappy over the manner in which he left his hometown club. Second-row Sims played three times for England on the 1998 'Tour of Hell' after making his international debut in the 64–22 thrashing against New Zealand.

He captained Gloucester under Richard Hill, but did not fit into the plans of his replacement Philippe Saint-André and exited Kingsholm for spells at Worcester, Bedford and Exeter.

Sims said: 'I loved playing at Kingsholm – the fans are the best in the world and have got real knowledge – I just wished I got the same backing on the pitch. I loved playing for the club, it was all I wanted to do and I didn't want to go.

'Richard Hill did a fantastic job and never got the credit he deserved. He built the side that had success later on.'

Sims was at the heart of the club as it made the transition from being amateur to professional. When he became the first full-time pro, part of his duties included helping out with administrative jobs in the office.

'I didn't really feel under pressure as the first full-time pro,' he said. 'But the advent of professionalism was quite hard and we were struggling.'

Now in his early 40s, Sims is still playing for Wellington while working as a sports technician at Exeter College. He added: 'The worst games for me were in the cup against Bath. I sat on the bench in the final when we lost heavily and didn't get on. When we played them in the semis I got concussed. Overall though, I've got more good memories than bad. The real supporters know I gave everything. I couldn't have given any more, but life goes on.'

WHERE ARE THEY NOW?

Second-row Peter Miles played for top clubs, Gloucester, Bath, Bristol and Cinderford. He now works in the world of high performance cars for Forge Motorsport.

BANISHED IN BRISBANE

Scott Benton was a crowd favourite in the 1990s, and was also a player/coach at Morley RFC. Scrum-half Scott made just 1 appearance for England, in the record 76–0 hammering at the hands of Australia in Brisbane in 1998. That defeat ruined plenty of England careers but it didn't do Phil Vickery too much harm. He played that day, as did Jonny Wilkinson, Austin Healey and Danny Grewcock.

ONE-CAP WONDERS

The following players appeared just once for England while with Gloucester.

Charles Smith v Wales	1901
Bumps Carpenter v South Africa	1932
Peter Hordern v Wales	1934
Ken Wilson v France	1963
Chris Williams v France	1976
Gordon Sargent v Ireland	1981
Malcolm Preedy v South Africa	1984
Richard West v Samoa	1995
Mark Mapletoft v Argentina	1997
Scott Benton v Australia	1998
Steve Ojomoh v New Zealand	1998

HAPPY AT HOME

Fred Webb captained Gloucester during the 1920/21 season, which saw Gloucester go unbeaten in 23 home games.

A DRUBBING TO SAVOUR

4 May 2002 is a date true fans will never forget because that is the day Gloucester thumped the old enemy Bath 68–12 at Kingsholm. Ironically, the Bath team that day contained Tom Voyce, Rob Thirlby, Gareth Delve, Gareth Cooper and Olly Barkley, as well as the likes of Steve Borthwick, Danny Grewcock and Mark Regan.

Gloucester destroyed them with tries from James Simpson-Daniel (three), Terry Fanolua (two), Henry Paul, Junior Paramore, Robert Todd and Patrice Collazo, plus 23 points from the boot of Ludovic Mercier.

… AND ONE TO FORGET

On 31 August 1996, Gloucester lost emphatically 75–19 at Harlequins. Ireland captain Keith Wood made his Quins debut in this match.

FINDING COURAGE

Marcus Hannaford was Gloucester's skipper when the Courage Leagues were first introduced in 1987. Gloucester finished fifth in the top division. Matches were arranged on mutually agreed dates between clubs and Gloucester's opponents during that breakthrough season were Bath, Bristol, Coventry, Harlequins, Leicester, Moseley, Nottingham, Orrell, Sale, Wasps and Waterloo.

Leicester Tigers won the league, with Coventry and Sale relegated. Rosslyn Park and Liverpool St Helen's were promoted to replace them.

Hannaford remained skipper the following season as Gloucester rose to second in the table. Matches were now scheduled on Saturdays. Hannaford said: 'When the leagues first started there was still probably more of an emphasis on the cup. We were in a position one year to do the double but lost out on both. We beat Nottingham in the semi-final of the cup but the following week we played them in the league and they [Nottingham] had much more urgency and beat us. We tried to regroup for the final but lost to Bath.'

Gloucester also finished second in 1989/90 under Mike Hamlin. It was 1994 before the league structure was expanded to include a full rota of home and away matches. Sky started showing live league matches in 1995.

AN EYE LIKE A TROPICAL FROG

Marcus Hannaford says a lot of the rough treatment he received off the ball spurred him on. 'A lot more things happened off the ball during the era I played and I took a lot of cheap shots from the opposition's blindside flanker and hooker. I had my jaw fractured versus Saracens. I didn't realise it was broken until I blew my nose and my eye blew up like a tropical frog. Apparently blowing your nose is the last thing you should do.'

Hannaford's father Bob and uncle Charlie both played for Gloucester. Marcus represented Widden Old Boys and Longlevens before making the move to Kingsholm. He made his debut versus Stroud away, then suffered a serious eye injury during his first home game against Newport.

Injuries plagued Hannaford during his fourteen seasons at Gloucester. He played on through the wear and tear but when the game went pro he realised he couldn't justify giving up time in the day for the money on offer.

He said: 'I missed out on an England cap because of injury. I was all ready to go when I got injured versus Coventry. Nigel Melville was injured and Richard Hill was out too so I would have played. I got injured at the wrong time. England went for Richard Harding instead, getting him out of retirement.'

Hannaford says the best try he ever scored came in an England shirt, for England B versus Italy. He also remembers scoring a memorable try at Welford Road against Leicester. He rates John Gadd as the best player he lined up alongside, and David Bishop as the best scrum-half he faced.

'If I was picking a dream Gloucester XV the first name on my list would be John Gadd. He was everything you wanted in a blindside forward, hard physically, he could sort out trouble but was also great with the ball. He worked well around the fringes, very much like Richard Hill, the England and Saracens player. 'David Bishop of Pontypool was a bad boy, but he could certainly play.'

Hannaford says he felt 10ft tall every time he pulled on the Gloucester shirt. He added: 'My seasons as captain were highlights but I also like to think I had an impact on the Anglo/ Welsh thing. When I first started going over the bridge to play in Wales if often felt like we were beaten before we got on the pitch. There were a lot of negative vibes and I couldn't get my head around that. It was tough. You'd get refs who were on first-name terms with the home team and the split decisions always seemed to go their way. One of the most incredible games was against Glamorgan Wanderers. Some of our boys got held up in traffic but the ref was adamant we should kick off with 12 players. Looking back, that's unbelievable.'

HOW ILLUMINATING

Floodlights were first installed at Kingsholm in 1967. The first match played under lights was against the Bosuns. Gloucester won the game 34–8.

THE THOUGHTS OF MIKE HAMLIN

Mike Hamlin played around 330 times for Gloucester, captained them in 1989/90 and 1990/91 and toured Spain with England B in 1989. He joined the club from Cheltenham in 1982 at the age of 23.

The former MEB worker still watches Gloucester, and has also helped out with some coaching at Coney Hill. He said: 'I watched Gloucester as a kid and it was fantastic to play at Kingsholm. It's a rugby city. The game now might be faster and quicker, but not harder. To play for Gloucester in any era you have to have a certain quality. We gave a lot of commitment. We'd train Mondays and Thursdays, play Wednesdays and Saturdays and combine that with work and family.

'I always thought the beauty of rugby was that you met people from all professions and all walks of life. I played behind great forwards and we played to our strengths. We had a very good record versus Leicester because we always knew if we beat them up front we could cope with them behind.

'Rugby now? There's still a lot of skill but it's often twenty or thirty phases of forwards picking up. You can't compete.'

51 GAMES UNBEATEN

Gloucester went 51 games unbeaten at home from 10 October 1970 to 23 September 1972.

POPULAR NAME

The Shed, now renowned throughout rugby circles, used to be known as the Popular Enclosure. The main grandstand opposite the Shed was first built in 1926, costing £2,500 and containing 1,750 seats.

KEVIN DUNN: IN HIS OWN WORDS

My best and worst matches

'Any time you beat Bath or Leicester, especially away, was memorable. I remember winning against Leicester at Kingsholm and Tim Smith missed every kick and the ref gave us nothing. I think we scored seven tries that day.

'I also remember beating Leicester at Welford Road with two pushover tries. Teaguey didn't score them though, on both occasions our scrum-half Lloyd Gardiner got the ball and dived over.

'The worst match was probably losing to Nottingham, which cost us the 1989/90 league title. I think that game was Brian Moore's last for Nottingham.'

My most embarrassing moment

'We were playing Bath in a cup semi-final in front of a full house at Kingsholm. I got so wound up before the match that I ran out of the dressing room straight into some galvanised railings. I couldn't breathe and I honestly thought I had cracked a rib. It took me 5 or 10 minutes to get into the game.'

Playing for England

'I toured Spain and New Zealand with England B and was on the bench twice for England, but I never got on. The first time was in 1988 when we beat Australia at Twickenham.

'The other time was at Wembley in 1991, while Twickenham was being rebuilt. It was against Canada, but John Olver was picked ahead of me. It would have been nice to have got a cap but back then a lot of good players at Gloucester didn't get a look-in. Teaguey did, but he was special. He was a bit like Lawrence Dallaglio, you looked at him in the changing room and you were glad he was on your side.

'I remember talking to Jack Rowell in a pub in Richmond after I had played for England B against Ireland B. He said "you shouldn't be here, you should be with the England side". Then he got the England director's job ... and picked Graham Dawe!'

My toughest opponents

'The best I played against were Tom Lawton of Australia and Dal Maso, the French hooker. The toughest in England was Graham Dawe. We had some real battles. When I first joined Gloucester in 1986 I had some fierce competition from Glynn Mann for the number two shirt. We came to blows in a trial match and I remember Matt Bayliss threatening to send us both off.'

IT'S A SQUAD GAME

In 2010/11, 38 players were used in Gloucester's first XV. Eliota Fuimaono-Sapolu made the most appearances, 19. Compare that with the centenary season of 1973/74 when Gloucester played 54 games (winning 39) and Mike Nicholls played in 52 of them.

Seventeen players played more than 19 games that year: M. Nicholls (52), R. Clewes (45), J. Spalding (45), P. Butler (43), A. Brinn (42), J. Haines (39), J. Fidler (35), D. Owen (34), K. Richardson (33), J. Jarrett (32), R. Jardine (29), R. Etheridge (29), T. Palmer (27), R. Redwood (25), R. Cowling (24), J. Watkins (22) and R. White (21).

TRUE ALL-ROUNDERS

Graham Parker played rugby, football and cricket for Gloucester sides in the 1920s and '30s. He was a Cambridge Blue in rugby and cricket and also represented the county cricket side. He played rugby for England in 1938.

Willie Jones played rugby for Gloucester and cricket for Glamorgan. He was arguably one of Glamorgan's finest all-time players, scoring more than 13,000 runs and taking 192 wickets. He made two double hundreds in the space of a fortnight in 1948, compiling 207 versus Kent and 212 versus Essex.

Probably the greatest cricketer to play rugby for Gloucester was Tony Lewis CBE, who scored more than 20,000 runs for Glamorgan, played nine Test matches for England and later became a leading BBC cricket broadcaster. Lewis captained the England cricket team on debut and led the national side eight times. His first Test was against India in Delhi in 1972 and he led England to victory with 70 not out in the second innings. At Kanpur in the Fourth Test he scored his only Test century, 125. He served as captain and chairman of Glamorgan CCC and president of the MCC.

Lewis played rugby for Gloucester from 1957 to 1959 while stationed at RAF Innsworth for his National Service.

OWZAT FOR VERSATILITY?

Gloucester Rugby Club used to run its own cricket team called the Cherry Pickers, which often played at Frampton-on-Severn against the likes of Gloucester City and Woodpeckers. Digger Morris was a frequent wicket-keeper.

GREAT SCOTS

Scrum-half Rory Lawson is the grandson of the late, great BBC rugby commentator Bill McLaren. Rory's father Alan was also a Scottish international scrum-half, while his brother Gregor played for London Scottish and the Scotland national sevens team.

SMITH RED-CARDED ON DEBUT

Ian Smith was only sent off once in his Gloucester career – on debut at the age of 18 against Rosslyn Park after coming on as a sub. He'd only been on the field 10 minutes when he was red carded for fighting.

Ian, the son of the great Dick Smith, captained the club from 1991 to 1994 and won 25 caps for Scotland. 'Because father was so involved with the club I remember watching a lot of the big games and lots of training,' said Smith.

'I even sat in the dugout as a kid for a Western Counties versus New Zealand game. When you went along to try out for Gloucester as a player you had to back yourself. You had to promote yourself. It was like you incurred the wrath of the community if you failed. It was a hell of a thing to do. A lot of people more than good enough never tried out because of that.'

Smith switched from Longlevens to Gloucester in 1982 and was a key figure at Kingsholm until 1997. He said: 'When I first started we used the old changing rooms. I can still remember the very old, traditional dark wooden panels, the smell of liniment, the smell of rugby. There was an old bath so big you could drown in it. The wooden corridors provided a lovely walk up to the pitch.'

Smith says there weren't a lot of support systems in place once a player had broken into the first XV. His dad helped him with a lot of technical stuff and so did his old Longlevens coach, Derek Cooke. In the United team, he watched and learned from men such as Jerry Herniman, John Watkins and Paul Williams, who were on the way down from the firsts.

Smith's breakthrough into the Scotland team came out of the blue, courtesy of his Scottish grandparents. He explained: 'It all came about after a game against Nottingham. I was chatting to Chris Gray in the bar and must have said something. Then Ian McGeechan rang me. I thought it was someone pulling my leg and it took him ages to convince me it was really him.'

Smith left Gloucester for Moseley in 1997 because 'Richard Hill wouldn't pick him'. He subsequently coached at Moseley for seven years and then at Hartpury College. He said: 'Gloucester was not a great recruiting club and when I took over as captain it was really the end of an era because a lot of blokes were finishing. Things work in cycles. I didn't get paid and didn't expect to. I played under Keith Richardson and my dad. It must have been difficult for him. I've got three sons and I wouldn't coach them.'

THIS PROP WILL TAKE YOUR TEETH OUT

Prop forward Tony Windo worked as a dental technician for more than a year after training with another former Gloucester player/dentist Paul Williams. Rugby must have been good for business!

Windo played more than 200 games for Gloucester before going on to play another 230-plus games for Worcester. Another product of Longlevens, he captained Gloucester Colts and made the step up to the seniors after being invited to go on tour with them to Portugal. He is now director of rugby at Bromsgrove Hall School, and Gloucester's scrum coach.

'A professional career nowadays is ten years,' said Windo. 'You see a lot of young lads get nasty injuries, you've got to be lucky.

'In my early days you had to earn your spurs. If you put your bag down in the wrong place in the changing rooms the chances are it would be chucked in the showers.

'I grew up watching Gloucester. I was very good friends with Simon Devereux and we'd be standing in the Shed at 10.00 a.m. some Saturdays just to get our spot. That's part of what makes Kingsholm so unique, there's a large section of standing support and people get to the ground early to get their places. It was different at Worcester. Everyone had a seat. I've never been a fan of rugby clubs playing in football stadiums because they're soulless. Part of Gloucester's success is its heritage with all the memorabilia. You walk into some grounds like the Madejski and you see Reading footballers on the walls.'

Many Gloucester fans feel Windo should not have been allowed to leave Gloucester. The player himself admitted he was disappointed to be let go. 'It was Philippe's second year and I think I'd played every game the year before. I also went on the England tour in 1998. It was not about the money but I felt the club was playing on my loyalty. I only ever wanted to play for Gloucester but Worcester came in with a better offer. It was nothing against Philippe – when we played against Sale and he was their director of rugby he came up to me and said letting me go was one of his worst decisions. That was nice of him. He didn't have to say it.'

Now a coach, Windo says the game has changed massively in recent years.

'Coaching at the top level is all about putting the fine details into things. With the lads it's about core values and getting them to enjoy the game. I think one of the reasons Saracens have been so successful is they've got the team spirit right and they socialise together. A lot of clubs have lost that team spirit. At Gloucester we'd all have a few beers together on a Thursday night after training.'

TONY WINDO'S TOUGHEST OPPONENT

'The South African Balie Swart. We played against Transvaal at home and for the first 20 minutes I felt like I'd been thrown into a washing machine.'

FRIENDS, ROMANS, COUNTRYMEN

In 2009 Anthony Allen and Iain Balshaw dressed as Romans for posters designed to fill window space in the city's empty shops.

ADORED BY NORTHERNERS

Many young fans might not know that Lesley Vainikolo is a massive rugby league legend in Bradford. Big Les grew up in Auckland, who he represented in the 1997 Super League Challenge Cup. The following year he played for the junior Kiwis. He started his professional rugby league career with Australian side Canberra Raiders, where he earned his 'Volcano' nickname. He came to England in 2002 to play rugby league for the Bradford Bulls, scoring a remarkable 112 tries in 105 appearances. In 2007 he was named in Bradford's team of the century.

He made his international debut for the New Zealand rugby league team in 1998, scoring 14 tries in 12 appearances. He switched rugby codes to play for Gloucester in 2007, following in the footsteps of fellow Bulls players Henry Paul and Karl Pryce. Vainikolo scored five tries on his Gloucester debut against Leeds Carnegie. Although eligible to play rugby union for Tonga, New Zealand and England, he chose the latter – making his international union debut against Wales in February 2008.

WHERE ARE YOU FROM?

Fifteen Gloucester players from recent times and where/when they were born.

Henry Trinder – Swindon, 1989
Jonny May – Swindon, 1990
Nick Wood – Swindon, 1983
Mike Tindall – Otley, 1978
Alex Brown – Bristol, 1979
Olivier Azam – Tarbes, France, 1974
Charlie Sharples – Hong Kong, 1989
Olly Morgan – London, 1985
Freddie Burns – Bath, 1990
Akapusi Qera – Suva in Fiji, 1984
Luke Narraway – Worcester, 1983
James Simpson-Daniel – Stockton-on-Tees, 1982
Brett Deacon – Leicester, 1982
Eliota Fuimaono-Sapolu – Apia, Samoa, 1980
Jordi Pasqualin – Sheffield, 1990

WONDERFUL WILLIE

Willie Jones kicked 17 drop-goals during the 1947/48 season, but lies second in the all-time drop-goal list with 38. Top of the pile with 41 is Mickey Booth.

SHORT STINT

Barry Corless left his job as coaching director in 1995 just twenty months into a five-year contract.

WHERE ARE THEY NOW?

Former full-back Audley Lumsden is a physics teacher at Lord Wandsworth College in Hampshire. One of the school's famous former pupils is Peter Richards, who played scrum-half for Gloucester. Richards is now a rugby commentator for ITV.

TEN THINGS YOU MIGHT NOT KNOW ABOUT PETER BUTLER

- He was born in Alvin Street in Gloucester.
- He made his Gloucester debut on a Wednesday night at Kingsholm against Moseley. Gloucester won 31–12.
- His uncle Bob was a Gloucester prop.
- Peter first played rugby at Crypt School where his games master was former Pontypool player Horace Edwards.
- Despite playing well in the semi-final, Butler was dropped from the 1982 cup final team that drew 12–12 with Moseley. Paul Ford got the nod ahead of him.
- He used to idolise Eric Stephens as a boy.
- He went to Birmingham University where he was initially ignored at the rugby trials and ended up playing for the university's thirds.
- He would often catch the bus into King's Square for home matches and walk to the ground.
- Butler scored 2,961 points for Gloucester and another 367 points in 31 matches for the county.
- He made his international debut for England against Australia at the Sydney Cricket Ground, kicking a penalty and conversion in a 16–9 defeat. His only other England cap came in a 33–9 loss against the French at the Parc des Princes.

INFLUENCED BY THE DON

Like many who played under him, Eric Stephens rates Mike Nicholls as Gloucester's greatest captain. Eric said: 'Mike was inspirational and probably the best captain I played under.

'Don Rutherford was probably the biggest influence on my career. He was the first to get us training together as a team. He also introduced formal training – until then we'd been left to our own devices when it came to fitness.'

Eric joined Gloucester as a centre in 1959/60, aged 20. He found it hard to break through and left to go to London for two years. He came back when Don Rutherford retired and began playing at full-back in 1966/67 under the captaincy of Gary White. At the same time he also took on the goal-kicking duties.

With 1,562 points to his name, Eric proved himself a true Gloucester match winner, but he never won an England cap. He said: 'I thought I was better than some who were picked for England, especially as the selectors were chopping and changing full-backs all the time, but I never got a trial.'

Eric believes kicking was much tougher in his era, adding: 'Balls are better nowadays and pitches too. You also kick off tees now. Like in golf, it's much easier when you tee everything up.'

FREE DRINKS FOR THE PACK

A famous quote attributed to Doug Ibbotson states: 'The holy writ of Gloucester Rugby Club demands first that the forwards shall win the ball, second, that the forwards shall keep the ball, and third, that the backs shall buy the beer.'

DON'T PUMP IRON, DRINK STOUT

Matt Bayliss only played 20 or 30 times for Gloucester's firsts, mostly on Wednesday nights in Wales when the regulars caught 'Severn Bridge flu'. Matt believes his thin frame stopped him from playing more games for the firsts. He said: 'Tony Day, the chairman of selectors, told me I wasn't big enough. Following Jack Fowke's advice I tried drinking Mackeson to bulk up, but I'd wake up no bigger, but with a headache. It's incredible to look back and think that no one ever suggested lifting weights, but I don't think we even had any at the club back then.'

Matt is still proud of the role he played in developing the United side, captaining them from 1968 to 1971.

'We got the side on its feet and I take a lot of pride from that,' he said. 'I was a good organiser and we made the team half decent. We went out and got players and invited people along to the club, such as Wes Hall, Colin Teague and Maurice Hamlin. I went to selection meetings but had no say on the firsts.'

Matt says Digger and Roy Morris and Mike Burton were big influences on him. 'Digger was a selector and a touch judge – he was a terrible homer on the line. He was a big, funny man who would shake your hand and make you cry by squeezing it so tightly. Roy was a good player and a lovely man but he had to live in Digger's shadow with some people telling him he wasn't as good as his father.'

Even the greatest of the Gloucester greats had to play for the United side from time to time. Matt remembers one occasion during his spell as skipper when both Mickey Booth and Terry Hopson were dropped from the firsts following a poor game versus Cheltenham. 'Boothy came up to me and said "Matt, you toss the coin and I'll do the rest."'

When an ear injury forced him to pack up playing, Matt became a referee and often took charge of the Gloucester trial matches.

'They could be very tasty,' he said. 'And they were difficult matches to ref – I remember John Bayliss chasing Dick Smith around the field in one of them.'

DID YOU KNOW?

Sheep used to graze on the Kingsholm ground during the summer in order to keep the grass down.

GLOUCESTER PERSONIFIED IN ROLLED-DOWN SOCKS

No player epitomises Gloucester Rugby Club better than Mike Teague. With socks rolled down beneath his ankles he was the archetypal working-class hero – a down-to-earth local builder who went on to conquer the sporting world.

Young Mike grew up watching Gloucester from the Shed before developing his own playing career with All Blues. He joined Gloucester at the age of 18 during the 1978/79 season, scoring a try on his debut against Exeter University. Teague went on to make more than 300 appearances for the city club, helping them to a share of the 1982 John Player Cup and Merit Table success in 1985/86.

His England debut came as a replacement in February 1985 in a 9–9 draw with France at Twickenham. His first start for England came on the 1985 summer tour of New Zealand where he figured in two defeats – an 18–13 loss in Christchurch and a 42–15 defeat in Wellington.

Teague fell off the England radar for three years after that, until being recalled for the 12–12 draw with Scotland in the 1989 Five Nations. He also played against Ireland, France and Wales. 1990 was a breakthrough season for England and

Teague's stature in the team grew. The Five Nations season culminated in a Grand Slam decider at Murrayfield, which the Scots won 13–7 with three Craig Chalmers penalties and a famous Tony Stanger try.

By 1991, Teague was an integral part of an England team that finally achieved Grand Slam glory with a 21–19 win over France at Twickenham. That side has gone into rugby folklore and even today, when pub conversations turn to England's best all-time back row, the names of Mike Teague, Peter Winterbottom and Dean Richards – ever present in that 1991 Grand Slam success – trip off the tongue. Teague scored the only try in England's 25–6 win over Wales (their first win in Cardiff for twenty-eight years) and he also touched down in the 16–7 victory over the Irish in Dublin. That same year, England reached the World Cup final, with Teague playing in 5 out of 6 matches in the tournament.

England lost the final to Australia 12–6 at Twickenham with Aussie prop Tony Daly scoring the only try of the game.

Teague only represented England once in 1992, versus South Africa at Twickenham in a special match that marked South Africa's return from exile to the international stage. His final England appearance came in a 17–3 defeat against Ireland at Lansdowne Road in March 1993.

In total, Iron Mike earned 27 England caps, scoring 3 tries.

Whatever he achieved with Gloucester and England, Teague will probably be best remembered for his achievements as a British Lion. He toured Australia with the Lions in 1989 but was ruled out of the First Test by a shoulder injury. The Lions were hammered 30–12. Teague returned for the Second Test and inspired the Lions to a famous comeback. They won 19–12 in Brisbane and 19–18 in Sydney to seize the series 2–1. Teague was named player of the series following two fantastic individual appearances. He played 6 times for the Lions on that tour and was never on the losing side.

He went on tour with the Lions again in 1993 to New Zealand. He was not selected for the opening Test, a 20–18 defeat at Lancaster Park, but made his last international appearance in Wellington, coming on as a replacement in a 20–7 victory. The Lions lost the series 2–1 following a 30–13 defeat in Auckland – with the selectors sticking to their preferred back-row of Ben Clarke, Peter Winterbottom and Dean Richards.

Picked six times for the Barbarians, Teague also toured South Africa in 1989 with a World squad and played in both tests to mark the centenary of the South African Rugby Board.

Teague had brief spells at Cardiff, Moseley and even Stroud, but played his final club game for Gloucester versus Harlequins at Kingsholm in 1995. He was appointed Gloucester's team manager the following season.

MIKE TEAGUE: IN HIS OWN WORDS

John Watkins

'Andy Ripley was a hero of mine when I was growing up, while Phil Blakeway and Richard Mogg were two men I played with who I admired hugely. My all-time Gloucester hero though, is John Watkins. He's definitely the most underrated. He was very similar in lots of ways to John Gadd, so honest, they would both always put the team before themselves.

'When I started out at Gloucester I was very keen. I can remember walking into the changing room just before a big cup game. They were all doing their table-thumping, getting ready to play. John Watkins was the captain – and I will always remember the way he spoke to me and made me feel welcome. I shouldn't have been there but he didn't belittle me or tell me to get out. He is such a modest man who achieved so much. He used to say things to me about what I had achieved in the game but very few people went with the England side and won in New Zealand and South Africa like him.'

Training

'I went through the Ivor Oakes training schedule under the wonderful guidance of Jerry Herniman. It was like army training, it was old school bash. Fantastic! You'd stand in the rain with your arms out to see who packed in first. It was all about mental toughness.

'The "Iron Mike" nickname was given to me by Paul Ackford. It was around the time Mike Tyson was fighting and came from the way they introduced the boxers ... "All the way from Gloucester, weighing in at 220 pounds ... it's Iron Mike Teague!" – it was that sort of thing.

'I did weight training, which was not so common back then. I did most of my training on my own. I honestly believe the weight training made me what I was and Dave Pointon was instrumental in helping me to get into it.

'When I first joined the club in 1978 or '79 they told me I needed to put 2 stones on, but I was just advised to drink Guinness and eat fish and chips. I also did mad dog training with a group of guys from Cinderford and it was the fittest I ever got. I still know all of those forest tracks.'

Why I joined Cardiff

'I went to Cardiff to try to get picked for England, but it went horribly wrong. John Scott the England number eight was there when I joined them and it seemed like a good opportunity, but I lost form and wasn't playing well.

'You've got to remember that Gloucester was an unfashionable club. To use a Mike Nicholls analogy, to get picked for England while at Gloucester you had to be three or four times better than everyone else. There were no easy passages and no committee men voting for you. Everything you achieved you achieved on merit.'

The best back row: Gadd, Longstaff & Teague versus Winterbottom, Teague & Richards?

'It was a privilege to play in both – two different types of back row. If they clashed it would be a close call, but I suppose on a good day England would just shade it.'

Career highlights

'Obviously, the pinnacles were being named player of the series for the British Lions, winning the Grand Slam in 1991 and reaching a World Cup final, even though we lost.

'At Gloucester, the highlight was playing in a pack with men like Preedy, Sargent, Mills, Blakeway, Gadd and Longstaff. That was an international class pack. One game that sticks in my mind is thrashing Leicester at Kingsholm through the sheer force of the pack. I remember we ran over the top of them at a ruck so fast and so powerfully that we went back and did it all over again. I think Leicester scored one try during that match and when they got it the crowd started singing "Happy Birthday".'

CAPTAIN MINE CAPTAIN

Gloucester skippers through the 1970s and the club's seasonal playing records:

1970/71 – Mike Nicholls – Played 51 Won 35 Drew 4 Lost 12
1971/72 – Mike Nicholls – Played 49 Won 37 Drew 3 Lost 9
1972/73 – John Bayliss – Played 53 Won 36 Drew 2 Lost 15
1973/74 – Mike Nicholls – Played 54 Won 39 Drew 4 Lost 11
1974/75 – Keith Richardson – Played 45 Won 32 Lost 13
1975/76 – Mike Burton – Played 53 Won 34 Drew 3 Lost 16
1976/77 – John Watkins – Played 53 Won 34 Drew 3 Lost 16
1977/78 – John Watkins – Played 49 Won 38 Lost 11
1978/79 – John Watkins – Played 48 Won 35 Drew 2 Lost 11

GETTING ONE OVER BRISTOL

On Saturday, 8 June 2002, Gloucester won the Zurich Championship final at Twickenham, seeing off Bristol Shoguns by 28–23.

The Championship final was the culmination of a controversial eight team play-off (offering a wildcard European place), which was announced midway through the season. Gloucester, led by coach Nigel Melville, edged this tight contest with some heroic forward play from the likes of Jake Boer, Rob Fidler and Patrice Collazo, although the latter went to the sin-bin for 10 minutes after grabbing Augustine Pichot by the throat.

The game came at the end of a very long season. However, Gloucester scrum-half Andy Gomarsall had a fine match, while Ludovic Mercier again showed his skill with the boot. He scored 23 of Gloucester's points with seven penalties and a conversion. Jake Boer crashed over for their only try after taking a short inside pass from Collazo.

The Bristol side that day included the likes of Julian White, who had a ding-dong battle with Gloucester skipper Phil Vickery, Neil McCarthy, Alex Brown, Michael Lipman and Felipe Contepomi. Straight after the match, Vickery darted off to join the England party that was flying out to Argentina.

Gloucester's winners: Henry Paul, Darren O'Leary, Terry Fanolua, Robert Todd, Tom Beim, Ludovic Mercier, Andy Gomarsall, Patrice Collazo, Olivier Azam, Phil Vickery (captain), Rob Fidler, Ed Pearce, James Forrester, Jake Boer, Junior Paramore. Replacements used: Chris Catling, Trevor Woodman, Chris Fortey, Craig Gillies, Koli Sewabu. Not used: Andy Deacon, Dimitri Yachvili.

DID YOU KNOW?

Gloucester ended the 2001/02 season by scoring an amazing 280 points in their final 6 matches. They edged out Bristol Shoguns 41–40 at the Memorial Stadium, thumped Bath 68–12 at home, before winning 50–17 at Leeds Tykes. A 60–9 home quarter-final win over Newcastle Falcons was followed by a 33–11 success at Heywood Road against Sale Sharks. The 28–23 Twickenham win over Bristol was the *coup de grâce*.

WHERE ARE THEY NOW?

Neil McCarthy, who played for Gloucester from 1997 until 2000, is now the academy manager at Leicester Tigers. McCarthy played for England at under-16, 18, 21 and senior level.

THE MIRACLE MATCH

In January 2003, Munster gave Gloucester a lesson in clinical finishing that they will never forget. The Irishmen needed to beat Gloucester by an unlikely 27 points to qualify for the quarter-finals of the Heineken Cup at Gloucester's expense. They pulled it off with a 33–6 victory, courtesy of a John Kelly try in the dying minutes. The true heroes were the formidable Munster pack.

Gloucester were let down by a stuttering line-out and problems in the scrums, while full-back Henry Paul had one of those days where nothing seemed to go right. Peter Buxton and Olivier Azam both had spells in the sin-bin.

Gloucester's team that day was: Henry Paul, James Simpson-Daniel, Terry Fanolua, Robert Todd, Thinus Delport, Ludovic Mercier, Andy Gomarsall, Rodrigo Roncero,

Olivier Azam, Phil Vickery, Rob Fidler, Mark Cornwell, Jake Boer, Peter Buxton, Junior Paramore. Replacements: Clive Stuart-Smith, Simon Amor, Tom Beim, Chris Collins, Andy Deacon, Adam Eustace, Andy Hazell.

DID YOU KNOW?

Before Gloucester's trip to Munster in 2003 every player was issued with their own personal CD with details of Munster's tactics.

LET'S HEAR IT FOR THE BOYS

What have Richard Jewell, Anthony Allen, Olly Morgan, Freddie Burns, Charlie Sharples, Jonny May, Ryan Lamb and Jack Adams got in common? They all scored their first tries for Gloucester at the age of 19.

James Simpson-Daniel was only 18 years and 278 days old when he got his first Gloucester touchdown, but that was 58 days older than Marcel Garvey.

IRISH DIDN'T WANT BOER

Jake Boer joined Gloucester in 2000/01 as a 25 year old because London Irish had not offered him a deal. A year later, he was made captain by Philippe Saint-André. 2002/03 was a great year for Boer, who scored 11 tries in 24 appearances, including two in a Heineken Cup game against Munster. He was named Zurich Premiership player of the year and supporters' player of the year.

In 2003/04 he played in 28 of 31 games and signed a deal to stay at the club until 2007. However, his form dipped in 2004/05 and he lost the captaincy. Injuries in 2005/06 limited him to 18 appearances, but he still managed six tries. In 2006/07 he captained Gloucester in their last game at Kingsholm before the bulldozers moved in.

BORROWED SHIRTS

The famous cherry and white shirts worn by Gloucester were, legend has it, originally borrowed from one of Gloucestershire's oldest clubs, Painswick. According to local folklore, the club's strip was originally navy blue. However, when they found themselves without a set of shirts for a particular match they borrowed fifteen red and white ones from Painswick and adopted the colours as their own.

SAINTS SUNK AT TWICKENHAM

Beating Northampton 40–22 at Twickenham on 5 April 2003 to win the Powergen Cup will go down as one of Gloucester's greatest all-time achievements. Nigel Melville's side was simply superb in a thrilling encounter. Paul Grayson gave the Saints an early lead with a penalty, but James Simpson-Daniel swooped on a loose Matt Dawson pass to grab the game's opening try. Ludovic Mercier converted, before following up with a smart drop-goal.

The Saints side was packed with internationals that day including the likes of Dawson, Steve Thompson, Ben Cohen and Nick Beal. They clawed their way back into the game when Rob Fidler was sin-binned. In the time Fidler was on the sidelines, Grayson kicked two penalties and converted a Beal try to put his side 16–10 up.

Back came Gloucester, with 19-year-old winger Marcel Garvey becoming the youngest try-scorer in the cup's history after good work from James Forrester. Mercier converted. The first half ended 22–20 in Northampton's favour after Mercier had kicked another penalty and Grayson two more.

In the second half Gloucester's forwards took a firm grip on the game with Forrester touching down and Mercier converting. TV cameras later indicated that Forrester may have lost contact of the ball when scoring.

Henry Paul, playing in the centre, was always a threat, and when Grayson tackled him off the ball he was yellow-carded. Two more Mercier penalties left the Saints trailing 33–22 and even when Grayson returned, it was Gloucester who had the last laugh. Mercier seized on another poor Dawson pass and raced into space, before releasing a scoring pass to James Simpson-Daniel. The reliable Mercier slotted another conversion.

Jake Boer captained Gloucester in front of a bumper crowd of 75,000, but generously sent Andy Deacon, the competition's oldest finalist, up to get the trophy.

Gloucester's winners: Thinus Delport, Marcel Garvey, Terry Fanolua, Henry Paul, James Simpson-Daniel, Ludovic Mercier, Andy Gomarsall, Trevor Woodman, Olivier Azam, Andy Deacon, Adam Eustace, Rob Fidler, Jake Boer (captain), Andy Hazell, James Forrester. Replacements used: Junior Paramore, Robert Todd, Ed Pearce. Not used: Clive Stuart-Smith, Simon Amor, Chris Fortey, Rodrigo Roncero.

TEN THINGS YOU MIGHT NOT KNOW ABOUT PHIL VICKERY

Phil Vickery is a Gloucester modern great who played 145 times for the club from 1995 until 2006, captaining them between 2001 and 2003. He won 73 England caps and

5 British Lion caps, touring with the Lions to Australia in 2001 and South Africa in 2009. He also played in three World Cups, 1999, 2003 as a winner and 2007.

- Born on 14 March 1976, Vickery left school at 16 to become a herdsman on his parents' farm.
- He is a qualified cattle inseminator.
- He made his England debut versus Wales at Twickenham in 1998 as a replacement for Darren Garforth.
- The 2011 *Celebrity Masterchef* winner said the pressure of being in the TV kitchens was the same as being on a rugby field. He clinched the coveted cooking crown by serving up a starter of scallops with black pudding, pea shoots, crispy parma ham and apple puree, followed by a main course of lamb fillet served with baby carrots, asparagus wrapped in mint, and parma ham and fondant potatoes. His dessert was orange and chocolate bread and butter pudding with clotted cream.
- He won 47 of his England caps while a Gloucester player.
- Vickery says he took up rugby because he saw his brother playing for Bude and getting drunk! Young Phil played for Bude Colts when he was just 13.
- Vickery played one season for Redruth.
- He captained England in the 2007 World Cup final. They lost to South Africa.
- In 2006 Vickery left Gloucester for London Wasps. He went on to earn the two medals missing from his trophy cabinet, a Premiership winner's medal (2008) and a Heineken Trophy medal (2007).
- His last ever game was fittingly for Wasps against Gloucester on 25 September 2010. A serious neck injury forced his retirement.

MOST CAPS FOR ENGLAND AS A GLOUCESTER PLAYER

47 – Phil Vickery
27 – Tom Voyce & Mike Teague
21 – Trevor Woodman
19 – Phil Blakeway
17 – Mike Burton & Andy Gomarsall

JOHN BRAIN: IN HIS OWN WORDS

John Brain was appointed Gloucester's operations manager in May 2011, bringing him firmly back into the Kingsholm fold after several years at rival clubs. Born and bred in Gloucester, John made nearly 300 appearances as a lock for his hometown club before dropping down a level to play for Bedford. He came back to Gloucester to serve as assistant coach to Philippe Saint-André before moving to Worcester, who he guided into the Premiership for the first time in their history. After that, he became Bristol's forwards coach, until taking a scouting job for Gloucester. John Brain sadly passed away in May 2012.

My playing days
'I played for Old Boys before joining Gloucester Colts in 1979. I made my first XV debut quite early versus Harlequins at Twickenham because there was a county game on the same day. Paul Ford also made his debut in the same match.

'Gloucester had a lot of good second-rows during my time at the club. There was me, John Orwin, Nigel Scrivens, John Fidler, Adrian Turton and a lad from Ross called Phil Winnell, who couldn't commit to playing regularly because he was a dairyman. He was an excellent player.

'The highlight of my career was the year we finished runners-up in both the league and cup. We were on for the double but lost the last two games to Nottingham and Bath. We were a very good side and had an excellent season but mentally and physically we were exhausted by the end of it.

'We beat a lot of good sides that year and it was a privilege to play in a side with the likes of Teague, Smith, Gadd, Mogg, Hamlin, Hannaford and Taylor. Nottingham did a job on us up front, but they were a useful side with people such as Gary Rees, Chris Gray and Simon Hodgkinson. Bath were three or four years ahead of everyone else in the way they prepared.'

On preparing for games

'Everything was laid out for us when we played, our shorts, shirts and socks were all pegged out properly but like I said, teams such as Bath were way ahead of us. We had no team meetings as such. We didn't even warm up on the field. Teaguey would turn up at twenty-five minutes to three for a three o'clock kick-off with his kit bag on his shoulder.

'Bath had people like Jack Rowell who actually coached the team and analysed the opposition. Pro rugby coaching was generally very much in its infancy in the 1980s and early 1990s.

'I left Gloucester for Bedford in 1992 even though they were a league below because I could see clubs such as Bath, Quins and Leicester progressing ahead of us on and off the pitch. We were stuck in the 1980s. My last game was the cup quarter-final versus Quins when I was 30 or 31. I just thought this club isn't going to win anything.'

Tom Walkinshaw

'His influence on the club cannot be overestimated. I was working with Philippe when Tom took the club on. Philippe had a very good relationship with Tom. I think people like Alan Brinn knew we needed to get an investor in – if we hadn't, we could have ended up where the likes of Coventry are now. With Tom Walkinshaw's backing, Gloucester kept pace with the pro era. When I came back the last time it felt like a different club.'

What rugby means to the city

'I watched Gloucester regularly as a kid and admired the likes of Burton, Brinn, Nicholls, Richardson, Stuart and John Dix and Paul Howell. Gloucester has been a rugby hotbed for a long time and the supporters still identify with the team. Gloucester has three things going for it, the cathedral, the rugby and its people. The people are a breed apart and they stop you from getting too big-headed. Gloucester, Leicester, Bath and Northampton are all rugby institutes with very strong identities.'

Bryan Redpath

'Although a lot of money was thrown at the team I thought Gloucester was in danger of losing its soul because a lot of players didn't understand that they were playing for an institution. Look at Leicester, they always keep coaching teams in-house. Gloucester didn't do that and I felt they lost something. Bryan Redpath never played for Gloucester but I think he had a very good understanding of what the club is all about and getting players to realise they were part of a community and playing for a community.'

The modern game

'Rugby is a far better game now than when I played. Stick the Betamax on from my era and it's embarrassing. The game has progressed in every sense. Players are fitter, faster, stronger and the game's pace and physical intensity is higher. A few people have tried to tinker with the game but we're still producing a good spectacle. The important thing is we stick to a set of laws where all shapes and sizes can play and where things like a strong scrum still get rewarded.'

WHERE ARE THEY NOW?

Robin Cowling, who made more than 300 appearances in Gloucester's front row, is now team manager of Exeter Chiefs. Cowling played in Gloucester's 1972 knockout cup win over Moseley. He won 14 England caps but didn't get the first of them until after he had joined Leicester in 1974.

CHALK AND CHEESE

In 1981/82 Gloucester lost only 3 games out of 48 under the leadership of hooker Steve Mills. It was a different story for Steve in 1982/83, as the club lost 25 of their 54 fixtures.

STEVE MILLS ON HIS DREAM FRONT ROW

If Steve Mills had to pick any one prop to scrum down alongside him in a battle he'd choose Mickey Burton. 'Burton was the best I played with, he was extremely clever,' said Mills, who joined Gloucester from Cirencester in the early 1970s.

'It's a pity you couldn't put his brain into the heads of some other props. On the other side I'd choose either Phil Blakeway or Gordon Sargent.'

Mills believes the thing that gave Gloucester the edge over many of their opponents was their mental toughness. 'We would always give as good as we got,' he said.

Though he played in the amateur era, Mills says for twelve years rugby was his job and work was his hobby. The computer operator made more than 300 appearances for Gloucester as well as 24 for the county. He won 5 England caps, captained England B and also represented the Barbarians. His Test debut came in May 1981 in a 19–19 draw with Argentina in Buenos Aires. John Fidler made his England debut in the same game.

Mills played his second Test against Argentina in Buenos Aires the following month, with England winning 12–6, but had to wait until February 1983 for cap number 3, a 13–13 draw with Wales. Steve Boyle was an England debutant in this international.

Mills played against South Africa in June 1984, with England losing 33–15. His final Test appearance came in November 1984, which resulted in a 19–3 loss at the hands of the Australians.

'Peter Wheeler of Leicester was usually selected in front of me,' said Mills. 'I was on the bench for England 20 or 30 times. In the early days, England training was not that great. We used Gilbert balls in matches yet would often train with Adidas or Mitre balls, which were completely different.

'A lot of things changed for the better under Bill Beaumont, who we called Bill "one more scrum" Beaumont because he always wanted to do a bit more.

'I enjoyed touring Argentina where I encountered the toughest opponents I ever faced.'

Mills says captaining Gloucester was a privilege.

'I had a lot of say on selection but didn't have to do much of the running around. My job was to create an atmosphere. Beating Leicester in the 1978 cup final was a highlight because myself, Burton and Sargent came of age that day.'

Hookers in the 1970s and 1980s generally had a lot more to contend with than they do now, according to Mills. He said: 'Throwing was tougher because there was no lifting in the line-outs. I threw to a 6in window whereas now they throw to about 3ft. I practised my throwing like a goal-kicker practises kicking. I would throw by the old clock at Kingsholm, or stand on the goal-line and try and hit the posts.

'When hooking I would often strike blind. You had to compete more than they do today and you had to have faith in your scrum-half. We scrummed a lot lower to the ground, you would be that low you'd have your face in the grass. But I think that was much safer. When the scrum collapsed you didn't have so far to fall.'

DID YOU KNOW?

Steve Mills might have played his last game for England in the 1984 Twickenham defeat against Australia, but that match launched plenty of other international careers including England's Stuart Barnes, Gareth Chilcott and Nigel Redman and Australia's Nick Farr-Jones. Ex-Gloucester coach Nigel Melville also became England's youngest ever skipper on debut in this game. He was 23 at the time. His record was subsequently broken by Will Carling, who captained England at 22.

FIDLERS ON THE HOOF

John Fidler

John Fidler made more than 400 appearances for Gloucester and won 4 England caps, 2 versus Argentina and 2 versus South Africa. Fidler started his rugby career with Cheltenham but joined Gloucester for the start of the 1970/71 season. He said: 'We had a very good side at Cheltenham and beat Gloucester home and away, but I knew that if I wanted to get on I had to play for Gloucester. When I joined the club Peter Ford said, "It's nice to have you but don't expect to play for the firsts this year". I played in a good United side and it was a decent springboard.'

Fidler was unlucky to play in an era when England were spoilt for choice for second rows. The former policeman, dubbed Officer Dibble by team-mates, said: 'People like Bill

Beaumont, Maurice Colclough and Nigel Horton were all around the same time as me. If I'd been Welsh I would've got 50 caps!'

Fidler was also Gloucester's team manager for five seasons after retiring from the game. He served under Richard Hill and Philippe Saint-André and was particularly close to the latter. Saint-André even lived with the Fidler family for three months.

Fidler said: 'It was great to play in a pack with people like Burton, Sargent, Brinn, Nicholls, Cowling, Watkins, Potter and Haines. We took no prisoners, we were feared and revered. The skulduggery that went on in games was amazing, there was so much physicality. We were nowhere near as fit as modern players but modern players don't have to go training before a night shift.

'I think rugby is generally going in the right direction and is still a good spectacle. Sky TV has got it right, but the game needs to be run by professional people. I hope we don't go down the same road as soccer over some things. I'm not a great fan of all the overseas players, personally I'd like to see as many local players as possible.'

Rob Fidler

Watching his dad play for Gloucester by his mum's side, Rob Fidler knew from a young age that there was something special about the sight, smells and sounds of Kingsholm on match day.

He started playing at the age of 12 at Whitefriars School, progressing through the Cheltenham set-up just like his dad had done. At 18, Rob joined Gloucester – ironically making his debut versus Cheltenham at his former home ground, the Prince of Wales Stadium. Phil Greening made his Gloucester debut in the same match.

Despite everything his father achieved in a cherry and white shirt, Rob still had to earn his spurs in his own right. He said: 'Because I came from Cheltenham and was a public school boy I was an outsider. Very often, it was me and seven lads from Gloucester in the pack. When I left it was very different, there were Samoans and Frenchmen.'

Fidler says beating Bristol in the 2002 Championship final was one of his most memorable games. The 2003 Powergen Cup final was equally memorable for hugely different reasons. 'I wasn't even named in the squad for that one and went out on the Friday night to drown my sorrows,' he explained.

'I was lying in bed at home on the Saturday morning when I got a call from Pete Glanville saying someone was not well and would I come down. I said "How serious is it? Give me a call back if you really need me." I got the call and ended up starting the game.

'A few of the boys I'd been out with on the Friday night were blinking their eyes on seeing me out there.'

Rob says his childhood heroes were his father and Bill Beaumont. The best he ever played with were Dave Sims, Ian Jones and Danny Grewcock. Fidler played alongside Grewcock after his shock switch to Bath. He explained that move by saying: 'It was just one of those things. I would have loved to have played my whole career at Gloucester but these things happen. Gloucester and Bath are very similar clubs. They are both very passionate rugby cities with rich heritages. I had five good years at Bath and never got much stick when I came back to Gloucester.'

Fidler says Richard Hill made Gloucester more professional in outlook, while Saint-André added some French flair to the mix. 'I think I enjoyed my rugby more towards the end with Philippe,' he said. 'You think things will last forever but you soon become too old. There aren't many people I even know at the club now, probably just Andy Hazell. I watch when I can but I'm still involved with Old Pats, coaching and playing a bit. You see the game now, the size of the players and the speed, and maybe it's a good thing I played when I did.

'There's a third generation of Fidlers coming through now and my son Ben is already playing for Old Pats juniors.'

Rob played twice for England, versus New Zealand in Auckland in June 1998 and against South Africa in Cape Town just over a week later. England lost that match with the All Blacks by 40–10. The All Blacks side contained the likes of Jonah Lomu, Andrew Mehrtens, Craig Dowd, Josh Kronfeld and Fidler's Gloucester pal Ian Jones. In the England second-row with him that day was Dave Sims. Fidler was also on the losing side against the South Africans, going down 18–0.

DID YOU KNOW?

John Fidler never lost a game against Bath throughout his career. His worst result against them was a 6–6 draw.

CINDERFORD WEREN'T ALWAYS PALS

Former Gloucester player Andy Deacon replaced another ex-Gloucester man, Pete Glanville, as director of rugby at Cinderford in 2010. In recent seasons the likes of Shaun Knight, Freddie Burns and Henry Trinder have all enjoyed successful spells at Dockham Road.

However, relationships between the two clubs were not so cordial back in 1923 when a number of players were injured in a particularly fierce clash at Kingsholm. The City Supporters' Club had arranged for a concert to take place that evening in honour of Cinderford's visit. However, the majority of people at the function were Cinderford supporters and the start was so late, most of them decided to go home.

Cinderford, seething from the way they had been treated, subsequently cancelled their next scheduled match with Gloucester – with the city club claiming they would have called the game off anyway.

ALL IN A DAY'S WORK

An assortment of Gloucester players from the early 1980s and the jobs they did for a living at the time.

Mark Calvert	policeman
Bob Clewes	building supervisor
Padraig Conway	engineer
Jim Delaney	engineer
Ron Etheridge	policeman
John Fidler	policeman
Jerry Herniman	policeman
Richard Jardine	policeman
Mike Longstaff	tax inspector
Steve Mills	computer operator
Dave Pointon	teacher
Malcolm Preedy	fitter
Colyn Price	insurance salesman
Gordon Sargent	insurance salesman
Adrian Turton	teacher
Kevin White	decorator
Ian Wilkins	teacher
Paul Wood	builder

POINTLESS

What do Karl Pryce, Carlos Nieto, Jon Pendlebury, Gareth Cooper and Jeremy Paul have in common? They all failed to get on the scoresheet for Gloucester despite more than 140 collective appearances.

Pryce's Gloucester career was particularly interesting. He was a high-profile signing from the Bradford Bulls rugby league team in 2007 but, despite joining on a three-year contract, played just 30 minutes in the Premiership against Newcastle Falcons.

WHERE ARE THEY NOW?

South African Thinus Delport was an early Nigel Melville signing in 2002, joining on a two-year deal from Natal Sharks. Delport is now a mentor for Sky Sports' Living for Sport initiative and goes around the country giving talks about rugby and life skills in schools. He is also a coach at Old Patesians RFC.

CAPTAIN MINE CAPTAIN

Gloucester skippers through the 1980s and '90s and the club's seasonal records:

1980/81 – Steve Mills – Played 51 Won 37 Drew 2 Lost 12

1981/82 – Steve Mills – Played 48 Won 41 Drew 4 Lost 3

1982/83 – Steve Mills – Played 54 Won 24 Drew 5 Lost 25

1983/84 – Gordon Sargent – Played 50 Won 33 Drew 1 Lost 16

1984/85 – John Orwin – Played 48 Won 32 Drew 1 Lost 15

1985/86 – John Orwin – Played 47 Won 33 Lost 14

1986/87 – Malcolm Preedy – Played 47 Won 30 Lost 17

1987/88 – Marcus Hannaford – Played 47 Won 32 Drew 3 Lost 12

1988/89 – Marcus Hannaford – Played 44 Won 34 Drew 1 Lost 9

1989/90 – Mike Hamlin – Played 47 Won 34 Drew 2 Lost 11

1990/91 – Mike Hamlin – Played 43 Won 32 Lost 11

1991/92 – Ian Smith – Played 36 Won 27 Drew 1 Lost 8

1992/93 – Ian Smith – Played 38 Won 28 Lost 10

1993/94 – Ian Smith – Played 41 Won 22 Drew 2 Lost 17

1994/95 – Andy Deacon – Played 39 Won 20 Drew 1 Lost 18

1995/96 – Dave Sims – Played 35 Won 18 Drew 1 Lost 16

1996/97 – Dave Sims – Played 42 Won 23 Drew 1 Lost 18

1997/98 – Pete Glanville – Played 41 Won 23 Drew 1 Lost 17

GIVE US A CLEWES

Bob Clewes scored 1,027 points for Gloucester and is one of only five men to play for more than 500 games for the club. The others are Dick Smith, Peter Ford, Alan Brinn and Richard Mogg.

PETER ARNOLD'S FAVOURITE GLOUCESTER PLAYERS

'My favourite has to be John Watkins. He had an uncanny feel for where the ball was going to go and his understanding with Peter Butler on restarts was amazing. Mike Teague was the best number eight and Watkins the best flank forward.

'Terry Fanolua was a tremendous character. When he tackled you, you stayed down. He had an excellent partnership with Richard "Skippy" Tombs in the centre, but Jardine and Bayliss were very good too. Jardine was a silky runner whereas with Bayliss it was a point of honour not to stay down and to get up before the other chap. John Bayliss tackled as hard as anyone I've ever seen.'

THE THOUGHTS OF ALLAN TOWNSEND

'My first game for Gloucester was in 1956 against Bucharest. It was very unusual to play overseas opposition on tour. I captained Gloucester in 1961/62 and it was an exciting time because our intake of youngsters included the likes of Mike Nicholls, from Old Centralians, John Bayliss, Dick Smith, Alan Brinn and Terry Hopson.

'When I was captain the likes of Tom Voyce, John A'Bear, Digger Morris and Mervyn Hughes were on selection. The bedrock of the club were the likes of Arthur Hudson, Doc Alcock and Tom Voyce.

'They were not intimidating figures at all because they let you have your say. I remember going round to see Doc Alcock in his flat in Cathedral Close and he made me very welcome. He was very approachable.'

Gloucester RFC president Allan Townsend was a tight-head prop who played 190 times for Gloucester. His work for a bank took him around the country and he also played for Aldershot Services, Bath United and Bournemouth.

BEST BAA BAA

Frank Stout played 24 times for the Barbarians, putting him joint fourth in the all-time Barbarians appearance list. Stout made his Barbarians debut in 1897 and played his final game in 1906. George Hastings played 20 times for the Barbarians from 1955 to 1959.

IRISH EYES NOT SMILING

In September 1991 Gloucester, coached by Keith Richardson, stunned the Irish President's XV by beating them 14–13 at Kingsholm. The Irish side contained most members of the national team, including Simon Geoghan, Nick Popplewell, Brendan Mullin, Donal Lenihan and Phil Matthews.

Jim Staples and David Curtis scored tries for the President's XV, with Ralph Keyes slotting a penalty and a conversion. Jerry Perrins and Simon Morris ran in tries for Gloucester, with Tim Smith knocking over two penalties. Gloucester hooker John Hawker claimed three strikes against the head while Dave Sims revelled in the line-outs against British Lion Lenihan.

That same month, Mike Teague led out the England side that took on Gloucester at Kingsholm. England, who like the Irish were preparing for the World Cup, won the match 34–4, but Gloucester gave a good account of themselves and managed a try through Derrick Morgan.

Jon Webb scored two tries and kicked four penalties and two conversions for England, with further tries coming from Chris Oti, Nigel Heslop and David Pears.

Gloucester team v Irish President's XV: T. Smith, J. Perrins, D. Caskie, S. Morris, N. Marment, Neil Matthews, M. Hannaford, Pete Jones, J. Hawker, Bob Phillips, P. Miles, D. Sims, P. Ashmead, I. Smith (captain), S. Masters. Replacements: R. Williams, A. Deacon, S. Devereux, B. Clark, L. Gardiner, D. Kearsey.

Gloucester team v England: T. Smith, D. Morgan, D. Caskie, S. Morris, N. Marment, M. Hamlin, R. Williams, Pete Jones, J. Hawker, Bob Phillips, N. Scrivens, D. Sims, P. Ashmead, I. Smith (captain), S. Masters. Replacements: Neil Matthews, D. Kearsey, M. Hannaford, A. Deacon, P. Miles, B. Fowke.

GADDY: ENGLAND'S LOSS WAS GLOUCESTER'S GAIN

Those who played with and against John Gadd cannot understand how he never won a single England cap. Admittedly, he played for England – scoring two tries in a 60–19 uncapped international win over Fiji at Twickenham in October 1982. However, nothing else followed.

'I think the England selectors saw both me and Mike Teague as blindsides,' said Gadd. 'Peter Winterbottom was about and Dean Richards was the blue-eyed boy. Gloucester were an unfashionable club.'

Gadd was born in New Zealand to English parents who emigrated. The family returned to England when John was 11. He went to Newent School and first played for Newent Colts at 16. His brother played in the same team. After a spell in the Newent second XV and a few games for the firsts the family moved to Gloucester and the young flanker joined Gloucester Old Boys. When he was 18 he caught the eye of Peter Ford.

'I was still 18 when I made my Gloucester debut versus Cheltenham in 1980,' said Gadd. 'I was in and out of the team that first year but John Watkins was a big influence and helped to bring me on. He even shifted to number eight to accommodate me. The city produced a lot of players for Gloucester back then and clubs like Matson, Old Boys and Gordon League all used to run four or five sides.'

Gadd relished the 'blood and guts' games that got the biggest crowds, like the home clashes with Pontypool. He rates Mike Teague and John Fidler as the best he packed down with. 'John was a father figure when I started out and you just felt safe with him around,' he said.

The low point of Gadd's career was getting sent off for stamping in the 48–6 cup final defeat to Bath in 1990. He didn't play much top level rugby after that. He was struggling with a knee injury, but continued to play for Stroud for several seasons. Today, he works for Magnox at Berkeley Power Station.

He said: 'When we were playing they told us we did things more professionally than we'd ever done before, but we didn't get any money. Other clubs looked after their players but Gloucester had old-fashioned attitudes. As players we never gave a thought to things like contracts and insurance. If we were successful we thought we might get a good job out of it. The world has changed.

'I watch some of the old games from the 1970s and '80s now and I think they look great. Rugby was much more off-the-cuff; we had a style but no hard and fast plans. We always played to win at Gloucester. Sometimes, playing the likes of Harlequins, they seemed happy with a jolly run about.'

WHERE ARE THEY NOW?

Centre Richard Tombs, one of the great signings following
the onset of the professional era, is a sales manager in New
South Wales, Australia. He plays veterans' soccer for fun!

BREAK IN CORNWELL

Mark Cornwell missed out on playing in the 2002 Zurich
Championship final after breaking his wrist. He subsequently
missed out on the chance to play in a Powergen Cup final
because of a stomach bug.

WOOLEY WOULDN'T GO AWAY

Viv Wooley's Gloucester career hardly got off to the best of
starts. He went from playing for Old Boys and training under
car lights to trying out at Kingsholm in the 1973 trials. 'They
told me to clear off because I wasn't good enough,' he said.

'In those days they still allowed anyone to train so I carried
on and kept trying to improve myself and get fitter.'

His determination paid off and in 1974/75 he made his
first XV debut versus Fylde. 'There were a lot of anomalies
I didn't understand,' he said. 'For example, you had to play
21 games in a season to be on the club photograph.'

Viv played for Gloucester from the early 1970s until
1981/82 but a knee injury (sustained against Pontypool)
curtailed his playing days at the top level. He went back to
Old Boys for a few seasons and obtained his coaching badges,
before returning to Kingsholm as a coach under Barry Corless.
When Corless left suddenly, Viv found himself temporarily in
charge until the arrival of Richard Hill.

VIV WOOLEY: IN HIS OWN WORDS

The 1978 John Player Cup and Gloucester's characters

'Playing for England under-23s meant a lot to me but I had tears in my eyes before the 1978 final. We stayed in the Richmond Hill Hotel on the Friday night and I remember we got lost going to Twickenham. We could see where we were going – I think the bus turned round once to follow the fans.

'We had some great characters in the team which is one of the reasons we were so successful. John Watkins inspired me. He was very quiet and never raised his voice. He wasn't a table-thumper but he made you listen.

'Phil Blakeway was another great character. I remember my grandfather died two days before a game at Kingsholm and I didn't want to play. Phil said "don't worry, I'll talk you through the game" and that's exactly what he did.'

My part in getting Phil Vickery to Gloucester

'Phil Vickery was very good friends with Phil Greening, I think they played together for England Colts. Phil Greening was in our 21s at Gloucester and he told me about Vicks. I said let's get him down for a weekend for a few beers.

'I met him on the Friday night and Phil Vickery stayed with Phil Greening's mum and dad. The initial contact with Phil Vickery was through me and Phil Greening. We introduced him to Gloucester.'

Mike Teague

'I flew over to New Zealand to watch the Lions when Teaguey was playing for them. We were in Waikato and after the game someone said to me "look there's Teaguey over there, aren't you going to say hello?"

'I said "I haven't travelled 6,500 miles to say hello to Teaguey – I can go up his house for a cup of tea any day of the week."'

The fans and the Shed

'I still live in Kingsholm and get the atmosphere just living here. Some criticise the people in the Shed but 99.99 per cent all know about the game and understand when people are trying or not. The Shed and the whole place is just tremendous. Every player, including me, cannot say thank you enough to the supporters.

'There was talk in the past about the club moving away from Kingsholm and relocating. A few of us were in the pub discussing it and someone said 'It would be like moving the cathedral. I hope it never happens. It would be sacrilege.'

SIGNING ON

When Craig Emerson joined Gloucester from Morley in 1996 he became the first player in England to leave one club for another for a transfer fee.

DEBUT IN SOUTH AFRICA

Lee Osborne's first XV debut for Gloucester was especially memorable as it took place in South Africa. Osborne was playing for his village club Berry Hill when he and team-mate Adey Powles were asked along to training at Gloucester towards the end of the 1993/94 season. The pair played one end of season game for the United XV versus Harlequins at Kingsholm.

The following season, the first XV squad was off on a pre-season tour of South Africa. Osborne was at work at the Xerox factory in Mitcheldean when he got a call from the club telling him that several players had dropped out of the tour and they needed him to go as a replacement.

'I was there like a shot,' he said. 'I couldn't get to Gloucester quickly enough to get measured up for my tour blazer.'

Osborne made his Gloucester debut in Cape Town against a team called Hamiltons. When he came back to England he hurt his shoulder in a warm-up game versus Lydney. He eventually made his home debut on the wing in a league game against Bristol. Osborne was an amateur player in an era when many of his team-mates were either semi-professional or professional. He left the club when Richard Hill took over as head coach, because he did not fit into his plans. 'I didn't really want to be a second-team player so I went back to Berry Hill,' he said.

'The highlights of my time at Gloucester were the games against Leicester and Bath in 1995. We beat Leicester 9–3 at Kingsholm and I scored all the points. We drew with Bath a month later.'

QUESTION & ANSWER SESSION WITH DON CASKIE

Don Caskie played in the centre for Gloucester from 1987 to 1999. Only 5ft 8in tall, he was a ferocious tackler and a crowd favourite. He now coaches the Georgia national team.

Can you recall the first time you walked into Kingsholm? Who was there to meet you and what were your first thoughts about the club?
'The first time I went to a training session the only other person there was John Hawker – we thought we had got the wrong day. Eventually everyone else arrived and I met Paul Williams, who made me feel very welcome. It was quite daunting but I was luckier than most since I had got to know a few of the players such as Mike Hamlin and Mike Teague from playing in various invitation sides. It meant that at least someone spoke to me in those first few weeks.

'I had known Keith Richardson since school – I was at Rednock in Dursley and he was a teacher at Wycliffe. Much to his annoyance we would regularly beat his school at rugby. When I went to college in London and joined London Scottish I would play against Gloucester. It was Keith who suggested that when I finished my degree I should come back and join the club.'

How did Gloucester differ from London Scottish?
'Gloucester was definitely a no-nonsense club. Everyone was very down-to-earth and you knew exactly where you stood. You had to earn the respect of your team-mates and a real team spirit was fostered. There was a real fear of failure, of letting your team-mates and the supporters down. The collectiveness of supporters and players made Kingsholm a very intimidating place to visit for opposing teams.

'London Scottish was much more happy-go-lucky. Big city jobs and big egos ... very much the cavalier attitude. On their day London Scottish were a match for anyone, especially in one-off cup games, but they never had the close club environment of players and supporters that makes Gloucester so strong.'

Within a year or so of joining Gloucester you played in a team that went close to pulling off the league and cup double. What do you recall about that season?
'There was a growing confidence around Kingsholm that this could be our year. A lot of players were hitting their best form at the same time. As it turned out the season proved to be just a couple of weeks too long for us. We were tired out and carrying injuries.

'We went into that final week on for the double but lost out on both and it was devastating, it took a long time to get over. Even after twenty years it still haunts me as a failure.'

Born in England to Scottish parents did you always regard yourself as Scottish? How did the other players view you?
'I had never really thought about my Scottish ancestry. I was brought up in Gloucestershire and went to Rednock School in Dursley. I went through the English schools' system and had an England final trial. It was only when I got to college in London that someone said to me that with a name like mine I must have a Scottish link. I was invited down to play at London Scottish and within a few months I had been selected for Scotland under-21s. The Scottish thing never really came up at Gloucester.

'Ian Smith, Pete Jones and myself were regarded just like everyone else. We were Gloucester players and that was our primary focus. Anything else that came along was a bonus. It was the same for all the players at Gloucester.'

Who did you like playing alongside most in the Gloucester midfield and why?
'I had the pleasure of playing alongside some great players at Gloucester. For me, the best was Richard Mogg. He had this knack of always being in the right place at the right time. His reading of a game was second to none. Being a relative youngster between him and Mike Hamlin was great. They were always talking to me, encouraging and offering words of advice. Both were very calming influences on the pitch.'

If you were picking your dream Gloucester XV, who would be first name on the team sheet and why?
'If pressed I would choose John Gadd, the epitome of the Gloucester spirit. Quiet, unassuming, but also ruthless and clinical. I never saw him once take a backward step – a very good man to have in your corner.'

Who was your boyhood rugby hero and why?
'Jean Pierre Rives was everywhere on the pitch and fearless – blonde hair all over the place – you couldn't miss him.'

Was it hard playing as an amateur at a time when many of your opponents were professional? How did rugby's transition from an amateur game to a professional one affect you personally?

'Professionalism only came in at the end of my career. The only decision I had to make was whether to give up the security of the day job or take the risk of maybe one year as a full-time player. Had I been younger then there would have been no question, but at 30 I had to be realistic, so I retired from Gloucester.'

How did the coaching job with Georgia come about and how is rugby viewed/developing in the country?

'I had known Richie Dixon for years. He was my coach for Scotland under-21s, Scotland B and Scotland A. He went on to become the Scotland national coach and director of rugby, overseeing coaching development. He kept a close eye on Ian Smith and myself when we were coaching at Cheltenham and Moseley and would pop down and see us.

'He then became head coach of Georgia and was asked to put a coaching team together to include taking them to the 2011 Rugby World Cup. He asked if we would both be interested in joining him. I said yes but unfortunately Ian could not commit at the time. However, he is now Georgia 's under-19s coach.

'Now the World Cup is over our attention has turned to development. I have been asked to set up the National Academy, providing a pathway for young players right up to the full national side and building the infrastructures and support systems that will maximise success at future World Cups. From the positive strides that were made at the 2011 Rugby World Cup, rugby has now overtaken football as the number one sport in Georgia.'

THREE WORLD CUP WINNERS

The England squad that won the World Cup in 2003 contained three Gloucester players, Phil Vickery, Trevor Woodman and Andy Gomarsall. Mike Tindall and Iain Balshaw were also World Cup winners but both played for Bath at the time. Tindall and Balshaw were two of the youngest members of the squad – the only player younger than them was Jonny Wilkinson.

DID YOU KNOW?

Terry Fanolua played in every backs position for Gloucester, bar scrum-half.

SUPER MAORI

Carlos Spencer was named at fly-half in the greatest all-time Maori XV by a panel of rugby experts in New Zealand. Spencer represented Gloucester in 2009/10.

HEINEKEN CUP ADVENTURES

European rugby has revolutionised the club game since the mid-1990s and Gloucester have certainly enjoyed many famous nights and plenty of cruel defeats on foreign shores. The first European Heineken Cup competition took place in 1995/96 but without any English teams. The English clubs joined the fray in 1996/97 but Gloucester had to wait until 2000/01 for their first involvement. They made a promising start by topping a pool that also contained Llanelli, Colomiers and Roma.

A 21–15 win over Cardiff at Kingsholm followed in the quarter-finals, thanks largely to a formidable pack effort from the likes of Kingsley Jones, Junior Paramore, Ian Jones and Rob Fidler.

Gloucester didn't manage a try in that match but fly-half Simon Mannix slotted six penalties and his replacement Byron Hayward kicked another. Sadly, Gloucester went out to old foes Leicester 19–15 in their semi-final clash at Vicarage Road. Five Simon Mannix penalties meant Gloucester were always in contention, but Leicester stole an edge with a try from Leon Lloyd (who went on to play for Gloucester), plus four penalties and a conversion from the boot of Tim Stimpson.

The Gloucester team that took on Leicester in that semi-final was: Byron Hayward, Rory Greenslade-Jones, Terry Fanolua, Jason Little, James Simpson-Daniel, Simon Mannix, Andy Gomarsall, Phil Vickery, Olivier Azam, Andy Deacon, Rob Fidler, Ian Jones, Jake Boer, Kingsley Jones, Junior Paramore. Replacements: Andy Hazell, Chris Fortey, Mark Cornwell, Chris Yates, Steve Ojomoh, Elton Moncrieff, Nick Cox.

In 2002/03 Gloucester finished third of four in Heineken Cup Pool Two behind Perpignan and Munster – losing out only on points difference. All three teams finished with four wins and two defeats in the group. Making up the numbers were the Italian side Arix Viadana.

The following season Gloucester and Munster were drawn in the same pool again. Both sides finished on 24 points (with 5 wins out of 6) to easily qualify for the knockout stages ahead of Bourgoin and Benetton Treviso.

Gloucester's involvement in the competition ended with a 34–3 thrashing at the hands of eventual winners London Wasps at Adams Park.

In 2004/05 Gloucester finished second in their pool behind Stade Français, but this time they failed to qualify for the knockout stages as only the best two pool runners-up went through to join the six group winners in the quarter-finals.

Gloucester came third in a pool featuring Leinster, Agen and Edinburgh in 2006/07, but greater success came in 2007/08 with 5 wins out of 6 putting the cherry and whites firmly on top of a group comprising Ospreys, Bourgoin and Ulster. Munster came to Kingsholm to spoil the party again in the quarter-finals, winning 16–3 with tries from Dowling and Howlett, plus two Ronan O'Gara penalties. Ryan Lamb kicked a solitary penalty for Gloucester.

A disappointing European campaign in 2008/09 saw Gloucester win 3 games and lose 3 to finish third in their pool with 15 points behind Cardiff Blues (27 points) and Biarritz (also on 15 points but with a better points difference). Whipping boys Calvisano failed to pick up a single point in the group.

In 2009/10 Gloucester came second in their pool, ahead of Glasgow Warriors and Newport Gwent Dragons, but again failed to make the knockout stages. They won 4 of their 6 matches to gain 17 points, but Biarritz topped the group with 23 points. The French side beat Munster to reach the final, but ultimately lost out 23–19 to rivals Toulouse.

THE COMPUTER KID

When Marcel Garvey signed a two-year deal with Gloucester in 2002 he kept his feet on the floor by continuing his computer studies course at Gloucestershire University in the evenings. Marcel's agent when he signed the deal was Mike Burton.

Marcel was quick on the pitch but he wasn't such a flyer under water. When Philippe Saint-André took charge he whisked his squad away to France for a team-bonding adventure trek. Because Marcel couldn't swim he had to be dragged through deep water by the guides who organised the trip!

THEY PLAYED FOR WIDDEN

Marcel Garvey is one of Widden Old Boys' favourite sons but he's not on his own. Others to have played for Widden and Gloucester include Adam Eustace, Marcus Hannaford, Ryan Lamb, Dave Spencer, Paul Webb, Paul Taylor, Chris Fortey, Brad Davies and Nathan Carter.

FIRST IN THE FRONT ROW

Gloucester became the first club to provide the entire front row for England when Malcolm Preedy, Steve Mills and Phil Blakeway were selected to play against South Africa in Port Elizabeth in 1984. England lost and the trio were dropped en bloc for the Second Test for Paul Rendall, Steve Brain and Gary Pearce. Preedy never played for England again.

MALCOLM PREEDY: IN HIS OWN WORDS

The sanctuary of the changing room

'I was born in Denmark Road and Gloucester had a conveyor belt of talent. I never thought I was good enough. When I went into the changing rooms for the first time the first person I saw was John Watkins. I wasn't sure what the score was so I asked him "any peg?" Those old changing rooms were special. The wooden floor was embedded with hundreds of stud marks and made you think about all the men that had gone before.'

My one England cap
'I don't know why I got dropped after the game against the Springboks, I thought I'd done OK. Me, Steve Mills and Phil Blakeway were all dropped but we had held our own. I remember the build-up to the game, John Scott, our captain, was playing in the second row, which wasn't his usual position. We only had two practise scrums because John said his ears were hurting. I wanted to practise more but I was the new boy so I went along with the seniors.'

Best captain
'I thought Mike Hamlin was probably the best I played under. He was in his comfort zone at Gloucester.'

Sponsorship perks
'The John Player Cup lost something for me when the new sponsors Pilkington took over – all the free fags we used to get! I used to smoke a pipe, mind you. I would get down the back of the bus with a bit of cherry and smoke everyone out.'

On Harlequins
'The Quins committee complained to the club about the state we were in when we got off the bus for a game. They said we looked like we had just walked off a building site, but most of us had. Our side was full of builders, chippies, plasterers and electricians.

'You only had to flick through the match programmes to see the difference between us and them. Our programmes had adverts from the corner shops around Kingsholm. Theirs were full of adverts from banks and airlines.'

My love of kicking
'I always fancied myself as a bit of a kicker. In a county final I whacked one into the corner from outside the 22 for Alan Morley to score. A lot of people also forget that I dropped a goal to win a game against Bristol 9–6.'

Malcolm Preedy captained Gloucester in 1986/87. He took up rugby at Hucclecote Secondary School and played club rugby for Longlevens.

SIX TRIES IN A GAME

Back-row forward Paul Ashmead once scored six tries in a single game for the United against Bedford. Ashmead also scored four tries in a game for the first XV against Coventry.

TRUE PALS

Fly-half Brian Russell joined Gloucester in 1978. He says the Lydney boys used to make him laugh. Brian said: 'There were four or five of them and they'd often travel up to training and games together, in one car. I remember one training session when Alan Brooks and Paul Howell arrived together. During training, Brooksy was offside and Howeller smacked him hard. Later on, they went off home together laughing and joking like nothing had happened.'

Brian remembers the infamous Gloucester versus Lydney clashes on Boxing Day. He said: 'None of the Gloucester boys really wanted to be there but for some reason all of the Lydney players did. They were always really pumped up. It was like it was their Christmas day.'

PAY TO PLAY

In 1969 Gloucester introduced a players' match fee of 2s 6d per player.

OOH LA LA!

Philippe Saint-André soon won the fans over with two tries on his Gloucester debut against Bristol in August 1997. The winger played 69 times for France, scoring 32 tries and captaining his country on 34 occasions. Only the great Serge Blanco has scored more tries for France (38). In his 31 Premiership appearances for Gloucester from 1997 to 1999, Saint-André managed 14 touchdowns.

EUROPE: THE SECOND FRONTIER

The European Challenge Cup (which has also been known as the European Challenge Shield and the Parker Pen Shield/ Cup) is Europe's second-tier competition. Gloucester have always featured prominently in this competition, winning it outright in 2005/06.

In 1996/97 they made a low-key entrance into Europe, managing only fourth spot in a six-team group. They finished in front of Ebbw Vale and London Irish, but trailed behind Bourgoin, Bordeaux Bègles and Swansea. The following season they topped a pool featuring Toulon, Beziers and Petrarca Rugby to earn a tough quarter-final tie away at Stade Français. They lost that match 53–22.

In 1999/2000 Gloucester finished 1 point behind Biarritz in their pool and just missed out on qualification for the knockout stages. Bridgend and Spain XV also competed in the pool.

Gloucester topped a group comprising La Rochelle, Caerphilly and Gran Parma in 2001/02, then crushed Ebbw Vale 46–11 in a Kingsholm quarter-final. They cruelly went down 28–27 to Sale Sharks in their semi-final encounter at Franklin Gardens. Terry Fanolua (two) and James Forrester scored tries in that match, with Ludovic Mercier adding 12 points with the boot.

In 2010/11 Gloucester failed to make the knockout stages after surprisingly finishing second in their group behind La Rochelle.

PETER JONES: IN HIS OWN WORDS

Prop forward Peter Jones made his Gloucester debut in 1982 and played his final game in 1998, the C&G Cup final versus Northampton. Another product of Longlevens, he was actually born in Arbroath, Scotland, but the family moved to Gloucester when Peter was 7. His father served in the navy. Although he was an England under-23s trialist in 1985/86, Peter won 1 cap for Scotland in 1992 in the 15–12 loss against Wales in Cardiff.

Playing for Scotland

'Looking back, I was one of the few in the Scotland team to be born in Scotland. I played 28 times for Scotland in total but only got 1 cap. I went to Tonga, Fiji, Samoa, Australia and France, four or five times. Commuting to Scotland was a killer – sometimes we'd do it three times per week. We would often fly from Birmingham or Heathrow, me, Ian Smith and sometimes Don Caskie as well.'

My bond with Ian Smith

'I played nearly all my rugby with Ian Smith – we were in the same sides at Longlevens and Gloucester. I liked the way he played. He captained Gloucester for three seasons during a difficult time when, as a forward, it felt like we had to win 85 per cent of the ball to win 3–0.'

The amateur ethos

'I liked a few drinks on a Friday night, nothing too heavy. Teaguey said "Jonah, you're playing great but think how much better you'd be if you didn't have a drink on a Friday." I never drank before a cup game with London Scottish and we lost. I thought "I'm not doing that again!"

'I think some players today have lost sight of the reason why they play the game. I'd like to see the money stopped for a month to see who turned up to play.

'I played with Bryan Redpath for Scotland and thought he was a very good signing for the club. He's a carpenter by trade, a working man, and he understood the old rugby ethos.'

The best Gloucester front rows

'My most enjoyable front-row was me, John Hawker and Bob Phillips. We played Harlequins with Jason Leonard and they'd been pushing everyone around. We had them in the air. Bob was a brilliant player, very underrated.

'We still have a natural abundance of front rows in Gloucestershire but we don't always make the most of them. Tony Windo had ten good years in him when he left. Not long back we had two kids in the England under-20s, George Porter and Shaun Knight. Somerville was in the firsts. We should have had those two lads learning and working with Somerville all the time. I think we missed a trick.

'I remember when we played Ireland, with Fitzgerald and Popplewell, and had them in the air. I also remember when England wanted a hush-hush scrummaging session with us before they played Wales. They came down on a Thursday night but it wasn't that hush-hush because 4,000 people were waiting for them. England beat Wales on the Saturday and Jeff Probyn said his Saturday afternoon was not as tough as his Thursday night. Jack Fowke was one of the great ones. I was friends with Gary Fowke and used to go round to Jack's to scrum down with him in the garden, with him kicking me in the shins!

'The toughest opponent I faced was Louis Armary of France. Playing against him was 80 minutes of hard work. You hit him and he kept coming back, no matter how hard you hit him. And he would hit you back.'

10 THINGS YOU MIGHT NOT KNOW ABOUT OLIVIER AZAM

· Born on 21 October 1974 in Tarbes, Olivier's mother and father met through rugby. Olivier's mother's brother played in the same team as his father Jean-Jacques and introduced them.
· He grew up on a farm close to the Pyrenees and started out as a number eight with his local side Tarbes before switching to prop and eventually hooker.
· He won the European Shield with Montferrand.
· His Test debut came in 1995 versus Romania at Tucuman. His final Test was against Australia in Melbourne in June 2002. Although he won 10 caps for France he only started three times for his country – his first and last appearances and once against New Zealand in Wellington in June 2001.
· Olivier played on the edge and was once banned for twelve weeks for kicking Saracens lock Steve Borthwick in the head. He got an eight-week ban for fighting with Newcastle's Epi Taione, a nine-week ban for gouging Jamie Roberts in the 2009 Anglo-Welsh Cup final and a four-week ban for headbutting Northampton's Adam Eustace (once a former Gloucester team-mate) in April 2011.

- Olivier made 239 appearances for Gloucester, scoring 27 tries. He made his club debut in a 34– 0 loss to Saracens at Vicarage Road in September 2001.
- He married wife Kate at St Audries Park, Minehead, in 2008.
- In 2010/11, Olivier became the first overseas player to be granted a testimonial by his club in the Premiership era.
- He opened the Armagnac restaurant in the Montpellier area of Cheltenham. Head chef Dan Richards previously played rugby for Wasps.
- After retiring in May 2011, Olivier took up a role as forwards coach with Toulon.

WHERE ARE THEY NOW?

Mark Mapletoft has come a long way since his early days at Gloucester, where he combined playing rugby with selling finance to farmers for the Barnwood-based firm FAF (the same firm that once employed Don Caskie). Mapletoft is now on the coaching staff at Harlequins, having served as national academy coach, working as part of the RFU's elite department under Rob Andrew.

He worked alongside Nigel Redman with the England under-20s, helping them to a Grand Slam and a Junior World Championship final place in 2008. The likes of Courtney Lawes and Ben Youngs have since gone on to the full England team.

Fly-half Mapletoft scored more than 400 points for Gloucester in the late 1990s. He toured Argentina with England in 1997 and won 1 cap in a 33–13 defeat in Buenos Aires.

TWICKENHAM BLUES

The 2009 Anglo-Welsh Cup final was a bleak day for Gloucester as they were destroyed 50–12 by a rampant Cardiff Blues side in front of more than 54,800 supporters at Twickenham. It was Gloucester's fourth successive Twickenham defeat.

Cardiff overpowered Gloucester up front and ran in seven tries through Leigh Halfpenny (two), Ceri Sweeney, Tom Shanklin, Ben Blair (two) and Tom James, plus six conversions and a penalty from the boot of Blair. Gloucester mustered a penalty-try, a Mark Foster touchdown and an Olly Barkley conversion.

Cardiff's backs were directed by Nicky Robinson, who joined Gloucester the following season.

Gloucester's team that day was: Olly Morgan, Matthew Watkins, James Simpson-Daniel, Anthony Allen, Mark Foster Ryan Lamb, Rory Lawson, Nick Wood, Olivier Azam, Greg Somerville, Alex Brown, Will James, Luke Narraway, Akapusi Qera, Gareth Delve (captain). Reps used: Scott Lawson, Carlos Nieto, Marco Bortolami, Andy Hazell, Gareth Cooper, Olly Barkley. Not used: Charlie Sharples.

NO SAVING CORPORAL RYAN

Former coach Dean Ryan was once a corporal in the Corps of Royal Engineers. As a player, Ryan represented Saracens, Wasps, Newcastle and Bristol, earning 4 England caps. It was at Bristol where he first cut his teeth as a coach – taking them to the 2002 Championship final, where they lost to Gloucester. Ryan subsequently joined Gloucester as assistant to Nigel Melville, before taking over as head coach in 2005 following Melville's departure.

Ryan left Gloucester by mutual consent in June 2009, following the embarrassing cup final defeat to Cardiff Blues and an end-of-season collapse that saw the team lose 4 games in a row to finish sixth – the club's lowest position for eight years, despite boasting a squad packed with internationals.

In seven years at Gloucester, Ryan won 143 games out of 230.

SOS: BACK ON THE BENCH

In October 2009 Andy Deacon agreed to return to Gloucester for one night only at the grand old age of 43. Coach Mark Cornwell found himself short of front row forwards for an A team game with Harlequins so he persuaded Deacon to go on the bench. Deacon was happy not to get on the pitch as Harlequins won the game 45–14. He did, however, return to Kingsholm in 2011 to play one final time in a charity game for Help for Heroes between the President's XV and the Combined Services.

Former drayman Deacon was the first Gloucester player to receive a testimonial. Always happy to give back to the grass-roots game, he once turned out for Longlevens III the week after he had played for Gloucester versus Bath. He played in the second row for Longlevens thirds that day, alongside Tony Windo, who had also propped for Gloucester against Bath the previous week.

THANKS DAD

Shaun Knight's father Adrian played for Gloucester and Worcester in the early 1990s. It was dad Adrian who converted his son from a back-row forward to a prop at the age of 14.

WHERE ARE THEY NOW?

Former second-row Nigel Scrivens keeps the Bee's Knees pub in Cirencester.

IT'S A MISMATCH

One of the most one-sided games ever seen at Kingsholm was the 106–3 win over Bucharest Oaks in the European Challenge Cup in October 2005. James Simpson-Daniel ran in four tries with others coming from Marcel Garvey (two), Rob Thirlby (three), Haydn Thomas, Nick Wood, Adam Eustace, Andy Hazell, Luke Narraway, James Forrester and Anthony Allen. Thirteen of the scores were converted, ten by Ludovic Mercier and three by Simon Amor.

There was another one-sided European clash with Italian side Viadana in 2002. Despite playing away from home in the Stadio Luigi Zaffanella, Gloucester won the game 80–28 with tries from James Simpson-Daniel (three), Terry Fanolua (three), Henry Paul (two), Jake Boer, James Forrester and Marcel Garvey. Ludovic Mercier added ten conversions.

In January 2002, Henry Paul scored 29 points and James Forrester a hat-trick of tries in a 99–0 triumph against Gran Parma.

PLAYERS OF THE YEAR 2001–11

2001/02	Ludovic Mercier
2002/03	Jake Boer
2003/04	Henry Paul
2004/05	Adam Balding
2005/06	Andy Hazell
2006/07	Andy Hazell
2007/08	James Simpson-Daniel
2008/09	Olivier Azam
2009/10	Gareth Delve
2010/11	Eliota Fuimaono-Sapolu

TOP POINTS-SCORERS 2001–11

2001/02	Ludovic Mercier, 334 points
2002/03	Ludovic Mercier, 255
2003/04	Henry Paul, 205
2004/05	Henry Paul, 136
2005/06	Ludovic Mercier, 213
2006/07	Willie Walker, 159
2007/08	Ryan Lamb, 158
2008/09	Olly Barkley, 125
2009/10	Nicky Robinson, 202
2010/11	Nicky Robinson, 147

TOP TRY-SCORERS 2001–11

2001/02	Junior Paramore & James Simpson-Daniel, 9 each
2002/03	Jake Boer, 9
2003/04	James Simpson-Daniel, 8
2004/05	Terry Fanolua & Marcel Garvey, 6 each

2005/06	James Simpson-Daniel & Peter Richards, 6 each
2006/07	James Bailey & James Forrester, 5 each
2007/08	James Simpson-Daniel & Lesley Vainikolo, 9 each
2008/09	Iain Balshaw & Olly Morgan, 9 each
2009/10	James Simpson-Daniel, 8
2010/11	Charlie Sharples, 8

CRUEL INJURY BLOW

James Forrester, a back-row forward with the speed of a winger, scored 51 tries in 134 appearances for Gloucester and looked destined to become an England regular until rupturing the anterior cruciate ligament joint in his knee in a game against Bristol in 2007 at Ashton Gate. He was forced to retire from the game in October 2008. Forrester subsequently became an investment broker, while also coaching Singapore Premiership outfit The Wanderers. He won 2 England caps.

EXTRA-TIME WIN OVER THE IRISH

Arguably the game that propelled James Forrester to the top of the European stage was the 2006 European Challenge Cup final against London Irish at the Twickenham Stoop, which Gloucester won 36–34 after extra-time. It was an enthralling contest. Forrester scored a 91st minute try to put his side back in front after Irish's Barry Everett had missed a drop-goal and a penalty. A James Simpson-Daniel interception try put Gloucester 12 points ahead with 15 minutes to play, but Irish hit back to level things up at 31–31 with two late scores. They seemed to have the momentum, but Gloucester dug deep and Forrester was first to get onto the end of his own fly kick with just inches to spare. Forrester later admitted the in-goal area was not as big as he had thought.

Gloucester led 18–13 at half time with tries from winger Mark Foster and flanker Andy Hazell. Ryan Lamb kicked two penalties and a conversion in the match, with Ludovic Mercier doing the same.

Gloucester's winners: Rob Thirlby, James Simpson-Daniel, Mike Tindall, Anthony Allen, Mark Foster, Ryan Lamb, Peter Richards, Patrice Collazo, Mefin Davies, Jack Forster, Jon Pendlebury, Alex Brown, Peter Buxton (captain), Andy Hazell, James Forrester. Replacements: Olivier Azam, Gary Powell, Adam Eustace, Luke Narraway, Ludovic Mercier, James Bailey, Haydn Thomas.

HAPPY JACK

Jack Forster, the farmer's son from Wigan, was just 19 when he won a European Challenge Cup winner's medal following Gloucester's win over London Irish. Big-hearted Jack gave his winner's medal to his dad Chris to say thank you for all the help he had given him over the previous years.

THE YOUNG AND THE OLD

The oldest players in Gloucester's squad during the past ten years (with their dates of birth).

2002/03	Andy Deacon	31/7/1965
2003/04	Andy Deacon	31/7/1965
2004/05	Christo Bezuidenhout	14/5/1970
2005/06	Mefin Davies	2/9/1972

2006/07	Christian Califano	16/5/1972
2007/08	Christian Califano	16/5/1972
2008/09	Olivier Azam	21/10/1974
2009/10	Pierre Capdevielle	30/3/1974
2010/11	Pierre Capdevielle	30/3/1974
2011/12	Will James	22/12/1976

And the youngest . . .

2002/03	Rob Elloway	9/11/1983
2003/04	Will Matthews	14/1/1985
2004/05	Ryan Lamb	18/5/1986
2005/06	Jack Forster	19/3/1987
2006/07	Jack Forster	19/3/1987
2007/08	Charlie Sharples	17/8/1989
2008/09	Freddie Burns	13/5/1990
2009/10	Freddie Burns	13/5/1990
2010/11	Freddie Burns	13/5/1990
2011/12	Gareth Evans	19/9/1991

DID YOU KNOW?

Chief executive Ken Nottage, now hugely respected in rugby circles, played top-level basketball for nineteen years and was one of the best players in England in the 1990s. He was the top scorer in the English League in 1992 and played more than 50 times for England. He got into rugby through basketball. He was working as a director for a university in the north-east when he was asked to develop a basketball team for Newcastle United, as part of Sir John Hall's sporting group, incorporating rugby, basketball and ice hockey. He progressed to become chief executive of the sporting group.

WE LV WINNING TROPHIES

Tries from Tom Voyce, Charlie Sharples, Eliota Fuimaono-Sapolu and Darren Dawidiuk earned Gloucester a deserved LV Cup success in 2011 and an easy 34–7 win over a weary Newcastle side at Franklin Gardens. Nicky Robinson converted all four scores and also added two penalties.

Gloucester led 10–0 at the break with a converted Voyce try and a Robinson penalty, but turned up the heat in the second period with the kicking of Nicky Robinson dictating terms. Despite being without many of their international players it was an impressive performance to secure the club's first trophy win in five years.

Gloucester's winners: Olly Morgan, Charlie Sharples, Tim Molenaar, Eliota Fuimaono-Sapolu, Tom Voyce, Nicky Robinson, Jordi Pasqualin, Nick Wood, Olivier Azam, Rupert Harden, Jim Hamilton, Alex Brown, Akapusi Qera, Andy Hazell, Luke Narraway. Replacements: Freddie Burns, Henry Trinder, Tim Taylor, Darren Dawidiuk, Shaun Knight, Will James, Matt Cox.

The LV Cup campaign got underway in November 2010 with an 18–12 defeat at Rodney Parade against the Dragons. Gloucester's points came via a penalty-try, a Lesley Vainikolo touchdown and a Freddie Burns conversion.

A thumping 36–10 win over Saracens got things back on track at Kingsholm. It was a victory to savour as Charlie Sharples, Henry Trinder (two), James Simpson-Daniel and Olivier Azam crossed the line for tries, with Tim Taylor adding 11 points with the boot. Most of the hard work was done in the first half as Gloucester raced into a 24–3 lead.

A 30–16 win at Leeds Carnegie put Gloucester top of Pool Three. Tom Voyce, Nick Wood, Lesley Vainikolo and Tim Molenaar scored tries, with Freddie Burns and Nicky Robinson each kicking a penalty and a conversion.

London Irish were then destroyed 41–8 at Kingsholm as Gloucester knew a win would put them into the semis.

They scored seven tries through Charlie Sharples (two), Akapusi Qera, Jim Hamilton, Olly Morgan, Tim Molenaar and a penalty-try, along with two conversions from Nicky Robinson and one from Freddie Burns.

In the semi-finals Gloucester blitzed Newport Gwent Dragons 45–17 at Kingsholm with star of the show Charlie Sharples running in four tries and Andy Hazell, Nicky Robinson and Eliota Fuimaono-Sapolu also touching down. Robinson kicked five conversions to round off a great afternoon for Bryan Redpath's men.

BUT THERE'S MORE PLAY-OFF HEARTACHE

After finishing third in the 2011 league campaign Gloucester suffered more play-off heartache with a 12–10 defeat at Saracens. Owen Farrell's penalty, 7 minutes from time, settled the outcome after Gloucester had thrown everything at their opponents. Nicky Robinson claimed all of Gloucester's points with a try, a conversion and a penalty.

PLAYING FOR PARAMORE

A team of former Gloucester players took on a Junior Paramore XV in December 2009 to raise money for the Samoan Tsunami Appeal. Members of Paramore's extended family were killed in the Tsunami.

Paramore first came to England to play rugby league for Castleford, before switching codes with Bedford and then Gloucester. Junior won Sky Sports' try of the month award for his effort versus London Irish in November 2002. He scooped more than half of the total vote. Gloucester players won the award in the two preceding months too, with

Marcel Garvey's hat-trick effort against Bristol being singled out in September, followed by an Olivier Azam touchdown against Saracens.

WORCESTER IS THE MODERN DERBY

Andrew Stanley was another local boy who would nip over the wall as a kid to get into the Kingsholm ground. He joined from Gordon League and developed under Dick Smith.

He said: 'The Gloucester I joined was quite a powerful club, there were around 15 internationals but only one or two players from outside the city. I was lucky enough to play in some fearsome packs. There was so much depth, we would bring people in from nowhere when necessary, like Barry Clarke, a farmer from Stow-on-the Wold, and they would immediately step up and do a brilliant job.

'For a spell, when he came on the scene aged 20 or 21, Pete Glanville was in my opinion easily the best blindside in the country. He was consistently good but never got a sniff of England.'

Stanley says the biggest rugby influence on him was Mike Nicholls, who drummed into him the responsibilities that came with playing for Gloucester. In his career, Stanley played more than 200 games for the club, retiring in 1998. He's now on the coaching staff at Worcester Warriors, who have become big Premiership rivals.

Stanley said: 'I still keep an eye on Gloucester and it's always good to go back. A lot of the backroom staff from my day are still there.

'A lot of people at Worcester have links with Gloucester, not just me but people like Marcel Garvey and Richard Hill. It does surprise me how Gloucester versus Worcester has blossomed into a real derby. The crowds at Kingsholm and Sixways create a great atmosphere. I still want Gloucester to do well, just not when they play us.'

SPLIT LOYALTIES

A Gloucester XV with one thing in common – they all represented Bath.

Backs: Freddie Burns, Ian Balshaw, Olly Barkley, Mike Tindall, Audley Lumsden, Terry Hopson, Andy Gomarsall.

Forwards: Allan Townsend, Terry Sigley, Keith Richardson, Dave Attwood, Rob Fidler, Peter Miles, Steve Ojomoh, Gareth Delve.

Coach: Richard Hill

DID YOU KNOW?

Big Jim Hamilton became the 1,000th man to be capped by Scotland when he made his debut versus Romania in 2006. Jim was actually born in Swindon and played for England under-21s.

He was a late developer who struggled to get into his school's first XV as a youngster. His break came out of the blue when he went to watch some of his Barkers Butts team-mates play for Warwickshire under-18s versus Leicestershire. A Warwickshire player got injured in the warm-up and Jim, despite nursing a hangover, ended up playing in the match. He must have impressed the watching Leicester coaching staff because he got invited along to Welford Road where he flourished as a rugby player.

Hamilton verbally agreed to join Stade Français before having a change of heart and opting to join Gloucester.

NO HIDING FROM OPTA

Opta have revolutionised the analysis of rugby matches, providing an unparalleled database of match stats. Here are some interesting Gloucester facts from the 2010/11 season:

- Rory Lawson made more passes than any other Gloucester player, 728.
- Nicky Robinson had an interesting season. He made more kicks from hand than any Premiership player (165), but was also joint top of the bad passes list with 18. Robinson also missed more penalties in 2010/11 than any other kicker, a total of 24.
- Jim Hamilton stole 11 line-outs, the fifth best figure in the Premiership.
- Charlie Sharples made more metres for the team than anyone. He was 10th best in the Premiership with 920 metres gained.
- With eight try assists, James Simpson-Daniel was Gloucester's best provider. He was second best in the Premiership, behind Ben Youngs of Leicester. Simpson-Daniel was the number one try provider in the country in 2009/10.
- Gloucester made 2,182 tackles, won 141 scrums and won 271 line-outs. Only Leeds and Harlequins won fewer scrums, but only Saracens won more line-outs. There were 300 turnovers conceded and 195 missed tackles.

DID YOU KNOW?

In 2006/07 Andy Hazell made more tackles than any Premiership player, a total of 211.

CAPACITY RISES TO ALMOST 17,000

On 11 September 2004, the new 3,000-capacity Buildbase Stand was opened for the game versus London Irish. It raised the capacity from 11,000 to 13,000. In 2007, work to demolish the grandstand got underway. The original stand, which opened in 1932, was replaced by a 6,000-seater stand that took the capacity close to 17,000.

Because of the redevelopment work, Gloucester played their 2007 home game against Bristol at Ashton Gate, home to Bristol City Football Club.

EUROPEAN HALF CENTURY

Gloucester's 50th game in the Heineken Cup came against Glasgow Warriors in December 2009.

SPEEDY LUDO

Ludo Mercier became the second fastest player in Premiership history to reach 500 points when he scored 24 points in the 29–22 win over Saracens.

TAKING ON THE WELSH IN A SING-SONG

The Churchdown Male Voice Choir sang the club's 'Gloucester Boys' song in front of more than 50,000 people, prior to the EDF Energy Cup final versus Cardiff Blues in 2009. They'd previously sung the song at Kingsholm many years before.

The lyrics to 'Gloucester Boys' are as follows:

We come from Gloucester, the pride of the west,
Some of the lads and some of the best,
We are respected wherever we go,
Where we come from nobody knows,
They call us the pride of the ladies, the ladies,
They spend all our wages, our wages, our wages,
We are respected wherever we go,
We are the Gloucester boys.

Maggie dear, a pint of beer, a woodbine and a match,
A tupenny ha'penny stick of rock, we're off to the rugby
    match,
To see ol' Gloucester score a try, the best in the land,
We are the Gloucester boys.

We are the Gloucester boys-oys, we are the Gloucester
    boy-oy-s,
We know our manners, we spend our tanners,
We are respected wherever, wherever we may go,
And when we are walking down the Kingsholm Road
doors and windows open wide,
You can hear the people shout 'put those ruddy Woodbines
    out!'
We are the Gloucester boys.

10 THINGS YOU MIGHT NOT KNOW ABOUT JAMES SIMPSON-DANIEL

· James attended the same Yorkshire school, Red House
  & Sedbergh, as Will Greenwood and Will Carling. The
  captain of his school side was Northampton's Phil Dowson.

- His younger brother Charlie was on Gloucester's books for a while and, like James, represented England Sevens.
- James scored his first hat-trick for Gloucester versus Bath in May 2002.
- He allegedly got his Sinbad nickname through his brother Chris, who was called it at school after the character in the former Channel Four soap *Brookside*. The name was passed down through the family.
- A keen horseracing fan, James, Mike Tindall and Nicky Robinson bought a gelding called Montbeg Dude at a bloodstock sale at Cheltenham Racecourse for £12,000 in January 2011. The horse was put into training with Michael Scudamore at Ross-on-Wye. Naturally, the owners' silks are red and white.
- His middle name is David and he was born on 30 May 1982.
- James has won 10 England caps but started only 6 of those games. His caps have come against Italy (2), New Zealand (2), Wales (2), Samoa, Australia, Ireland and South Africa.
- He was an usher at Phil Vickery's wedding and a groomsman at Mike Tindall's wedding. At his own wedding, Vickery, Tindall and Trevor Woodman were ushers.
- James has scored 3 tries for England: versus Italy at Twickenham in March 2003, against Italy in Rome in February 2006 and versus South Africa in Bloemfontein in May 2007. Ironically, that match against the South Africans was his last capped international.
- James joined Gloucester straight out of school after starring for England under-18s. He made his debut as a replacement at Northampton but scored a scorching 50-metre try on his first appearance at Kingsholm versus Rotherham in the 2000/01 season.

DID YOU KNOW?

Former World Cup winning prop Trevor Woodman MBE is a patron for International Animal Rescue.

NO MONEY FOR HAZELL

When Gloucester first went professional, Richard Hill advised Andy Hazell that there was no money for him so he should sign on the dole, train with the firsts and give it three or four months. It wasn't long before Hill was offering Hazell his first pro contract.

THROUGH THE ALPHABET

A selection of recent performers and their try scoring records (as at October 2011)

Anthony Allen – 22 tries in 91 appearances
James Bailey – 13 tries in 66 appearances
Mark Cornwell – 13 tries in 198 appearances
Gareth Delve – 4 tries in 56 appearances
Adam Eustace – 12 tries in 242 appearances
Terry Fanolua – 54 tries in 222 appearances
Jon Goodridge – 14 tries in 82 appearances
Andy Hazell – 24 tries in 246 appearances
Will James – 3 tries in 104 appearances
Seti Kiole – 1 try in 12 appearances
Ryan Lamb – 15 tries in 85 appearances
Ludovic Mercier – 14 tries in 105 appearances
Carlos Nieto – 0 tries in 66 appearances
Henry Paul – 19 tries in 116 appearances

Akapusi Qera – 22 tries in 81 appearances
Peter Richards – 18 tries in 55 appearances
Apo Satala – 2 tries in 30 appearances
Robert Todd – 8 tries in 60 appearances
Tom Voyce – 11 tries in 53 appearances
Willie Walker – 6 tries in 64 appearances

DID YOU KNOW?

Prop Rupert Harden first came to Gloucester's attention when he played in a National League One game for Tynedale against a Cinderford side containing Mark Cornwell and Andy Deacon. His father is Australian and his mother English. Harden was born in Australia but raised in England.

BONNY SCOTS

Since Ian Smith and Pete Jones made their full Scotland debuts in 1992, the likes of Rory Lawson, Alistair Dickinson, Scott Lawson, Chris Paterson, Jim Hamilton and Ally Strokosch have all represented Scotland while with Gloucester.

However, before Messrs Smith and Jones, Gloucester had only ever supplied one player to Scotland in the first 119 years of the club's history – D. Crichton-Miller, who made his Scotland debut versus Wales in 1931.

The first Gloucester player to play for Wales was J.A. Gwilliam in 1953.

Incredibly, no Gloucester player has ever represented the full Ireland team.

RODRIGO'S HEALING HANDS

Rodrigo Roncero was offered a Gloucester contract after paying his own airfare to take part in a pre-season tour of South Africa. The Argentinian prop, who is a qualified doctor, represented Gloucester from 2002 to 2004.

WHERE ARE THEY NOW?

The road from university to Kingsholm is now well trodden, but back in the 1990s it was unusual for a player to step straight out of college into the top flight. Full-back Chris Catling did just that when he arrived at Gloucester from Exeter University in 1996.

Catling was a crowd-pleaser who played the game as it should be played. Safe under the high ball and tough in the tackle, he liked nothing better than to daringly run the ball back with interest. Catling played 91 times for Gloucester between 1997 and 2003 but his try count of 22 was superb, showing his prowess at joining the line. His rugby career saw him play at the top level in England, France and Italy.

He is now head of operations in the UK for Deltatre Media – a sports data and technology firm who provide sporting results services for events and organisations, including on-screen graphics and live tracking systems. He joined the company after originally providing consultancy for the 2007 Rugby World Cup.

KINGSHOLM IS A FORTRESS
BUT AWAY WINS ARE SCARCE

In recent times Kingsholm has been an absolute fortress for Gloucester, but it's been much harder for the cherry and whites to win away. In 2002/03, 2006/07 and 2010/11 Gloucester didn't lose a single home match in the Premiership.

Collector's items: Home Premiership losses 2000–11

2000/01	Sale 18–19
	Bath 21–22
	Northampton 12–15
	London Wasps 3–28
2001/02	Leicester 18–40 (15 September 2001)
2002/03	None
2003/04	Bath 14–20 (8 November 2003)
	London Irish 29–35
2004/05	London Wasps 17–27
	Leicester 13–28
	Bath 19–24
	Northampton 18–26
	Leeds 15–33
	Saracens 13–14
2005/06	London Irish 9–13
	London Wasps 32–37
	Bristol 15–20
	Bath 15–18
2006/07	None
2007/08	Leicester 13–20
	Leicester (home semi-final) 25–26

2008/09   Leicester 8–20
            Worcester 6–13

2009/10   Northampton 14–27
            London Wasps 6–35

2010/11   None

Collector's items: Away Premiership wins 2000–11
2000/01   Rotherham 23–29
            Newcastle 18–19
            Sale 16–24

2001/02   Sale 21–44
            Harlequins 6–18
            Bristol 40–41
            Leeds 17–50

2002/03   Harlequins 19–25
            Newcastle 19–22
            London Irish 19–40
            Northampton 13–16
            Saracens 22–29
            Bristol 21–38

2003/04   Harlequins 0–16
            Leicester 18–28
            Rotherham 21–35
            Saracens 8–16

2004/05   Leeds 16–21
            Northampton 12–18
            Worcester 13–18
            Leicester 13–20
            London Irish 12–13

2005/06	Bristol 9–41
	Saracens 9–19
	Newcastle 9–13
	Leeds 7–31

2006/07   Harlequins 21–31
Worcester 24–33
London Irish 11–22
Northampton 5–7

2007/08   Leeds 24–49
Saracens 31–38
Leicester 17–30
Newcastle 13–20
London Wasps 17–25

2008/09   Bath 17–21
Saracens 21–25
Bristol 10–29

2009/10   Leeds 10–26
Worcester 22–23

2010/11   Bath 3–18
London Wasps 9–10
Northampton 16–18

BLOODED IN BATH

Tom Voyce, Dave Attwood, Tim Molenaar, Darren Dawiduk, Eliota Fuimaono-Sapolu and Pierre Capdeville all made their Gloucester debuts in the same game versus Bath at Kingsholm in September 2009. Gloucester won 24–5. It was also Bryan Redpath's first league game in charge.

A FITTING FINAL WORD . . .

'Ninety per cent of the guys were married when I played but we never saw our wives. We spent all our time together. We meet up every now and then and because there was such a bond, it's like we've never been apart. We just pick up where we left off.

'I can't describe what it's like to play at Kingsholm, it's just brilliant. I used to get such a buzz, the hairs on the back of my neck would stand up. It makes you understand the buzz footballers must get running out in front of 60,000-plus crowds.

'When you leave Gloucester, nothing is the same. It's like having a limb taken off. It's something that cannot be replaced.'

Jim Breeze on what it really means to play for the cherry and whites.